Robert Jackson is a
military historian. F
books on the subject, including the widely
acclaimed *Royal Air Force in Action* and *NATO
Air Power*.

Robert Jackson

ACES' TWILIGHT
The Air War in the West, 1918

SPHERE BOOKS LIMITED

SPHERE BOOKS LTD
Published by the Penguin Group
27 Wrights Lane, London W8 5TZ, England
Viking Penguin Inc., 40 West 23rd Street, New York, New York 10010, USA
Penguin Books Australia Ltd, Ringwood, Victoria, Australia
Penguin Books Canada Ltd, 2801 John Street, Markham, Ontario, Canada L3R 1B4
Penguin Books (NZ) Ltd, 182–190 Wairau Road, Auckland 10, New Zealand

Penguin Books Ltd, Registered Offices: Harmondsworth, Middlesex, England

First published in Great Britain by Sphere Books Ltd 1988

Copyright © 1988 Robert Jackson

Printed and bound in Great Britain by
Richard Clay Ltd, Bungay, Suffolk

ACES' TWILIGHT

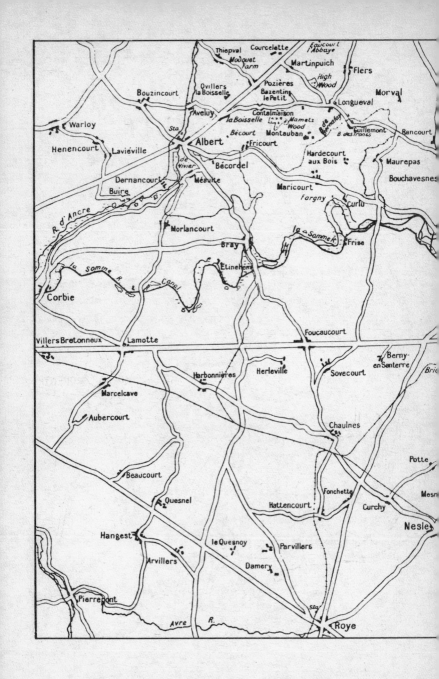

THE SOMME BATTLEG

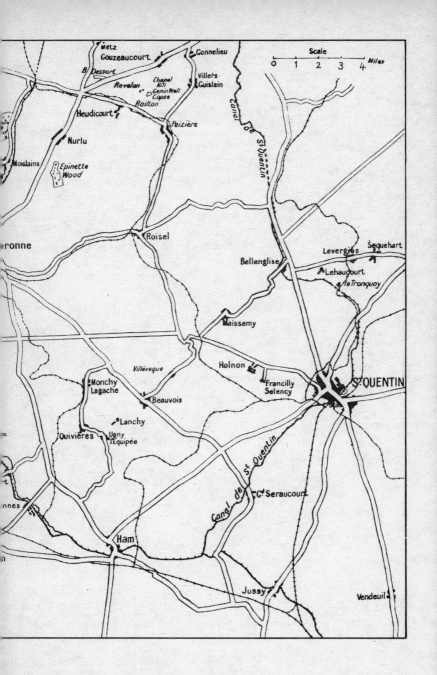

CHAPTER ONE

Georges Guynemer, the frail, almost sickly pilot who had risen like a meteor to become France's ace of aces with fifty-four victories, was dead.

Those who had seen him on that last day, a hazy September morning in 1917, recalled that he had seemed particularly nervous, pacing up and down anxiously while his mechanics prepared his aircraft for flight. He had been scheduled to fly a patrol with three other pilots, but two were late in arriving and so Guynemer, impatient as ever for combat, had decided to fly with only one companion, Lieutenant Bozon-Verduraz. They had taken off together for an airstrip near Dunkirk in their SPAD S.VIIs, on whose sides was painted the white marabou insignia of *Escadrille* SPA 3 – *L'Escadrille des Cigognes*.

Less than two hours later, Bozon-Verduraz returned alone. There had been a dogfight, and he had lost sight of Guynemer. His combat report told the terse story:

'Pilot: Bozon-Verduraz. Take-off time: 08.35. Time of landing: 10.25. Maximum altitude: 5,900 metres.

'At 09.25, together with Captain Guynemer, attacked an enemy two-seater over the lines at Poelcapelle. Made one pass and fired thirty rounds. Captain Guynemer continued to pursue the enemy as I was obliged to break off to avoid eight single-seaters, which were preparing to attack me. I did not see Captain Guynemer again. At 10.20, attacked a two-seater at 5,900 over Poperinghe. Fired ten rounds at point-blank range, then gun jammed. Pursued the enemy, but was unable to clear the stoppage and returned to base.'

The hours went by. Guynemer was long overdue. Commandant Brocard, commanding officer of the *Cigognes*, spent all morning on the telephone, searching for news; there was none. Then, in the afternoon, there came a message from an infantry unit to say that a French aircraft had been seen diving into the

1

German lines, although as yet there was no confirmation that it was Guynemer's.

The first hint of Guynemer's fate came three days later, when a German newspaper carried the report that Guynemer had been shot down by a German named Captain Wissemann, but it was to be another month before the news was officially confirmed. In response to a note sent via the Spanish Embassy, the Department of Foreign Affairs in Berlin issued the following statement:

'Captain Guynemer fell in the course of an air flight at 10.00 am on 11 September last, close to Cemetery of Honour No II to the south of Poelcapelle. A medical examination revealed that the index finger of the left hand had been shot away, and that the cause of death was a bullet in the head.'

Some time later on that September morning, the British artillery laid down a heavy barrage on the area where Guynemer was said to have fallen. After the brief examination by a German patrol soon after the crash, the pilot's body had been left in the wreckage. After the barrage, a second patrol was sent out to bring in the remains, but they found no trace of either pilot or aircraft on the smoking, shell-cratered ground. Both had been completely obliterated.

A week or so after the death of Georges Guynemer, Captain Wissemann, who claimed to have shot him down, wrote home to his family: 'Don't worry about me. Never again will I meet an adversary who is half as dangerous as Guynemer.' Only nineteen days after writing those words, Wissemann was himself shot down and killed by a man who was destined to emerge from the holocaust of the First World War as the top-scoring Allied fighter pilot. His name was René Fonck.

Fonck, who had scored his early victories over the terrible battleground of the Somme in 1916 and who had joined the *Cigognes* in April of the following year, soon began to establish his position among the ranks of France's leading aces. In October 1917, in the course of thirteen and a half hours' flying time, he destroyed ten enemy aircraft using fairly simple tactics. He would fly high, so that he was almost always above his opponents; then, choosing his moment carefully, he would use

2

his height and speed advantage to gain surprise. His aim was excellent, and a single firing pass on the dive was usually enough to send down his enemy.

By the end of 1917 Fonck's score stood at nineteen enemy aircraft destroyed, putting him in equal third place with two more talented pilots, Captains Albert Deullin and Georges Madon. In second place was Captain Alfred Heurtaux, with twenty-one, and leading the field was Lieutenant Charles Nungesser, the senior surviving French pilot with thirty victories.

The British, too, had lost their ace of aces in the bitter air fighting of 1917. Early in the year, the score of Captain Albert Ball DSO, MC, the rising star of No 56 Squadron, Royal Flying Corps, had been running neck and neck with that of Georges Guynemer, and the newspapers had been quick to seize on the friendly rivalry that had been growing between the two. At the beginning of May 1917 Ball had actually passed Guynemer's total, and there had been much speculation about whether he would catch up with the leading German fighter pilot, Manfred von Richthofen, who at that time had fifty-two kills to his credit.

Ball and No 56 Squadron had skirmished with von Richthofen's *Jagdstaffel* 11 on several occasions, but Ball had never made contact with von Richthofen personally. Then, in May 1917, the British learned that von Richthofen had gone home on leave and that his unit had been taken over by his brother, Lothar; it seemed an ideal opportunity to bring *Jagdstaffel* 11 to combat and, in the absence of its normal talented commander, inflict some losses on it.

In the evening of 7 May 1917, therefore, two Royal Flying Corps squadrons – one of them No 56 – set out to mount an offensive patrol over *Jagdstaffel* 11's airfield at Douai. One of 56's pilots, Cecil Lewis, described the scene:

'The May evening is heavy with threatening masses of cumulus cloud, majestic skyscapes, solid-looking as snow mountains, fraught with caves and valleys, rifts and ravines . . . Steadily the body of scouts rises higher and higher, threading its way between the cloud precipices. Sometimes, below, the streets of a village, the corner of a wood, a few dark figures moving, glides into view like a slide into a lantern and is then hidden again . . .

'A red light curls up from the leader's cockpit and falls away. Action! He alters direction slightly, and the patrol, shifting throttle and rudder, keep close like a pack of hounds on the scent. He has seen, and they see soon, six scouts three thousand feet below. Black crosses! It seems interminable till the eleven come within diving distance. The pilots nurse their engines, hard-minded and set, test their guns and watch their indicators. At last the leader sways sideways, as a signal that each should take his man, and suddenly drops . . .'

As the fight was joined it suddenly began to rain, cutting down the visibility. The section leaders of No 56 Squadron tried hard to hold their men together, but in the confusion of the dogfight the squadron became badly dislocated. Some of the SE5s ran for home, others headed for a pre-arranged rendezvous over Arras. There, Albert Ball joined up with another flight commander named Crowe and the two continued their patrol, joined by a lone Spad. Near Loos, Ball suddenly fired a couple of Very lights and dived on a red-and-yellow Fokker Triplane, following it into a cloud.

It was the last time that Ball was seen alive. Of the eleven SE5s that had set out, in fact, only five returned to base.

On the German airfield at Douai, the Germans were celebrating. Not only had Lothar von Richthofen returned safely to base in a damaged aircraft, but he claimed that he had shot down Albert Ball. The claim was incorrect, and to this day controversy still surrounds Ball's death. He was either shot down by a German machine-gun mounted on a church steeple, or became disorientated in low cloud and went out of control. The Germans buried him near Lille, and dropped a message to that effect over No 56's aerodrome. A month later, it was announced that Ball had been awarded posthumously the Victoria Cross. His score of enemy aircraft destroyed at the time of his death was forty-three. Like Guynemer, he was just twenty-two years old.

It was the action of No 56 Squadron which, later in 1917, brought about the death of the second top-scoring German pilot after Manfred von Richthofen. He was Lieutenant Werner

4

Voss of *Jagdstaffel* 10, who by the time he went on leave early in September 1917 had achieved forty-seven victories.

Within a couple of hours of his return to duty on 23 September, Voss took off in his Fokker Triplane and went looking for another victim. The triplane had first made its appearance over the front early in September and, in the hands of experienced pilots such as Voss and Richthofen, was a formidable opponent. Nevertheless, it was not invincible; Lieutenant Kurt Wolff, the leader of *Jagdstaffel* 11 and an ace with thirty-three victories, had been shot down and killed in one on 5 September by Flight Sub-Lieutenant N. MacGregor of No 10 (Naval) Squadron, flying a Sopwith Camel.

Voss's victim on this first sortie of 23 September was a de Havilland DH4, which he caught and shot down as it was heading towards the British lines. On his way back to base he experienced some engine trouble, so he turned his usual aircraft over to the mechanics and got another machine ready for the next sortie. It was similar to his own in every respect apart from the colour scheme, which was silver-blue with a red nose.

At 6.00 pm, despite poor visibility, Voss took off in company with two Albatros Scouts, which then formed the main equipment of *Jagdstaffel* 11. Over the front line they saw an air battle in progress between a variety of British and German aircraft, including the SE5s of No 60 Squadron. Voss immediately manoeuvred into position to attack one of these, which was flown by Lieutenant H. A. Hamersley and which had become isolated from the others.

Twenty minutes earlier, six SE5s of 'B' Flight, No 56 Squadron, had taken off from their airfield at Estrée Blanche to carry out an offensive patrol. The flight was led by Captain James B. McCudden, who was accompanied by Lieutenants G. H. Bowman, A. P. F. Rhys-Davids, K. Muspratt, R. Maybery and R. T. C. Hoidge. Almost as soon as the SEs arrived over the front, McCudden spotted an enemy two-seater and attacked it, sending it down in flames. Re-forming his flight immediately, he then climbed hard to intercept a formation of six Albatros Scouts, slipping along just under the cloud base.

At that moment, McCudden sighted Hamersley's lone SE fleeing for its life, with Voss in hot pursuit. Abandoning the Albatros formation, he went after the triplane in a diving turn, followed by Arthur Rhys-Davids. The pair closed in rapidly on the German, one on either side, and began to open fire in short bursts. Voss, with four more SEs coming down fast to join the other two, took the only course of action open to him: he decided to turn and fight, doubtlessly hoping that the Fokker's manoeuvrability would enable him to hold his own until reinforcements arrived. He stood the Fokker on its wingtip and pulled round in a steep turn to face his attackers, firing as he came.

McCudden, taken completely by surprise, took the first burst through his SE's wing and broke away sharply. At that moment, a red-nosed Albatros DV arrived and joined the battle. Its pilot, almost as skilful as Voss himself, took on the task of protecting Voss's tail, and with his assistance the German ace abandoned his purely defensive tactics and got in some damaging shots at the SEs that were trying to out-turn him. For ten minutes the six SEs and the two German machines gyrated around the sky, the Germans looking out all the while for the expected help that would enable them to escape. It never came, and the outcome was inevitable. The combat report of Lieutenant Rhys-Davids describes the last frantic minutes of the fight:

'The red-nosed Albatros and the triplane fought magnificently. I got in several bursts at the triplane without apparent effect, and twice placed a new drum on my Lewis gun. Eventually I got east of and slightly above the triplane and made for it, getting in a whole Lewis drum and a corresponding number of rounds from my Vickers. He made an attempt to turn in and we were so close that I was certain that we would collide. He passed my starboard wing by inches and went down. I zoomed, and saw him next with his engine apparently out, gliding east. I dived again and got one shot out of my Vickers. I reloaded, keeping in the dive, and got in another good burst, the triplane effecting a slight starboard turn, still going down. I had now overshot him, zoomed, but never saw him again.'

McCudden, having broken off the fight for the moment to change an ammunition drum, saw the triplane's last moments. It seemed to stagger for a brief period, flying erratically; then it went into a steep dive, streaming smoke, and exploded on

6

impact with the ground. A few moments later it was joined by the red-nosed Albatros, destroyed by the other SEs.

Later, James McCudden wrote of Voss: 'His flying was wonderful, his courage magnificent, and in my opinion he was the bravest German airman whom it has been my privilege to see fight.' But perhaps the feelings of the British pilots were best summed up by young Rhys-Davids himself, the man who had ended the career of the 'Hussar of Krefeld', as Voss was nicknamed. As his colleagues gathered round to congratulate him, he shook his head sadly and murmured, as he set his glass aside: 'Oh, if only I could have brought him down alive!'

Such were the young men who, in that year of 1917, brought new skills and tactics to the embryo science of air warfare, and often paid the price of experimentation with their lives. Early in 1917, the problem of making good the severe losses suffered by the Royal Flying Corps (RFC) during the previous year had seemed almost insurmountable; in an effort to fill the gap, the War Office had ordered regimental commanders to appeal for volunteers for transfer to the flying service. Hundreds came forward, and at the same time the first Commonwealth volunteers also began to arrive. They were led by the Canadians, who, by special arrangement with the United States, had done most of their flying training in Texas and already possessed a high degree of skill.

The steady influx of these new personnel during the first weeks of 1917 did much to raise the morale of the RFC as it strove to gather its forces to meet the demands that would be imposed upon it by the coming spring offensives. These demands were dictated, first and foremost, by the continual need for effective air reconnaissance and artillery observation. Since the slow two-seat observation aircraft had to be protected, this requirement in turn gave rise to the development of offensive fighter tactics, designed to gain air superiority over an area of considerable depth behind the enemy lines and secure the observation machines, as far as possible, from interference by hostile aircraft. Also in 1917 came the growing realization that the aircraft was a highly effective weapon for harassing enemy troops and communications, and with it the development of bombing and ground-attack concepts.

The first Allied offensive of 1917 involved a major French

attack on the Aisne while the British pinned down a large part of the enemy forces in the north, the main objective in their sector being the capture of Vimy Ridge. The offensive began on 17 March and ended on 4 April. The First and Third British Armies were supported by twenty-five RFC squadrons, about half of them equipped with single-seat fighters. During this battle a new British combat aircraft, the Bristol F2A Fighter, made its operational debut. Fifty F2As were built; powered by a 190 hp Rolls-Royce Falcon engine giving it a top speed of around 115 mph and armed with a centrally-mounted synchronized Vickers gun and a single Lewis mounted in the rear cockpit, the first examples arrived in France with No 48 Squadron towards the end of March.

The squadron had only six Bristols in operation at the time of its arrival at its new base, Bellevue, and they were rushed into action before their pilots had time to get used to them or to develop proper tactics with them. At first they were flown like previous two-seaters, orientated around the observer's gun as the primary weapon, and losses were heavy. During their first patrol on 5 April, six Bristols led by No 48 Squadron's CO, Major W. Leefe Robinson VC (who had earlier distinguished himself by shooting down the German Shütte-Lanz airship SL11 at Cuffley on 2 September 1916) encountered five Albatros DIIs led by Manfred von Richthofen. The British pilots adopted the standard two-seater tactic of turning their backs on the enemy to allow their observers to bring their guns to bear. It was a serious mistake, and four of the six – including Leefe Robinson, who spent the rest of the war in a prison camp – were shot down.

Later, in an interview with a Berlin newspaper, Richthofen was openly contemptuous of the British machine, with the result that many German pilots came to regard the Bristol Fighter as easy game – with fatal consequences to themselves. When flown offensively, in the same way as a single-seat fighter, it proved to be a superb weapon and went on to log a formidable record of success in action. Several hundred Bristol Fighters were ordered in 1917, these being the F2B version with a 220 hp Falcon II or 275 hp Falcon III engine, wider-span tailplanes, modified lower wing centre sections and an improved view from the front cockpit. The F2B eventually served with six RFC squadrons – Nos 11, 20, 22, 48, 62, and 88 – on the Western Front, as well as with No 67 (Australian) Squadron in Palestine, No 139 Squadron in Italy and in the United Kingdom with Nos 33, 36, 76 and 141 Squadrons on home defence duties. The pilot who perhaps did most to vindicate the Bristol Fighter was a Canadian, Lieutenant Andrew McKeever, who destroyed thirty enemy aircraft while flying F2Bs, his various observers shooting down eleven more.

Another new type to enter RFC service in the spring of 1917 was the SE5 single-seat fighter, which was delivered to No 56 Squadron in March. Powered by a 150 hp Hispano-Suiza engine, the aircraft had a maximum speed of 120 mph. Armament comprised a synchronized Vickers gun firing through the propeller and a drum-fed Lewis mounted over the wing centre section. Although less manoeuvrable than either the French-built Nieuports or Spads, the SE5 was faster and had an excellent rate of climb, enabling it to hold its own in combat with the latest German fighter types. The SE5s of No 56 Squadron flew their first operational patrol on 22 April 1917.

The original SE5 was followed into service, in June 1917, by the SE5a, with a 200 hp Hispano-Suiza engine. The type was first issued to Nos 56, 40 and 60 Squadrons, and by the end of the year had been delivered to Nos 24, 41, 68 and 84. Deliveries were slowed by an acute shortage of engines, but the pilots of the units that did receive the SE5a were full of praise for the aircraft's fine flying qualities, physical strength and performance. It is probably no exaggeration to say that, in most respects, the SE5a was the Spitfire of the First World War.

It certainly had none of the vicious tendencies of the Sopwith Camel – although in fairness, once the Camel had been thoroughly mastered it was a superb fighting machine, and in fact it was to be credited with the destruction of more enemy aircraft than any other Allied type before the conflict ended. Early production Camels were powered either by the 130 hp Clerget 9B or the 150 hp Bentley BR1 rotary engine, but subsequent aircraft were fitted with either the Clerget or the 110 hp Le Rhone 9J. Armament comprised twin Vickers guns mounted in front of the cockpit, and four 20-lb Cooper bombs could be carried under the fuselage for ground attack. The first unit to receive Camels was No 4 Squadron Royal Naval Air Service, followed by No 70 Squadron RFC, both in July 1917.

Delivery of the SE5 and the Camel came too late to prevent heavy RFC losses, which continued to mount steadily during the spring of 1917. There were three main reasons for the growing casualty rate. First, the RFC was still critically deficient in adequate combat aircraft; secondly, the prevailing westerly wind – which tended to carry the mêlée of air combat deep into enemy territory – was in the Germans' favour; and thirdly, the RFC insisted on maintaining an offensive policy throughout, no matter what the cost. Faced with superior enemy aircraft, it inevitably suffered an increase in losses because of this. By April 1917 new pilots were being sent to the front with as little as seventeen and a half hours' flying experience, which precipitated a vicious circle: the more inexperienced the British pilots, the higher the success rate of the German fighter squadrons. By the middle of 'Bloody April' 1917 the average life expectancy of an RFC pilot in France had dropped to two months.

During the first week of April 1917 the RFC lost seventy-five aircraft in action, mostly victims of an emerging band of tough, resolute German air fighters nurtured in the traditions of Germany's first air aces and fighter tacticians, Oswald Boelcke and Max Immelmann. At their head was Rittmeister Freiherr Manfred von Richthofen, and other German pilots were potentially just as dangerous to the Allies: men like Bruno Loerzer, the leader of *Jagdstaffel* 26, who destroyed ten British aircraft during the Battle of Arras and who was to end the war with forty-five victories. More than two decades later, the highly experienced Loerzer would command Luftflotte II during the Battle of Britain. Then there was Werner Voss, the brilliant Jewish ace (what would his fate have been, one wonders, had he survived the war to experience the Nazi regime?); Erich Loewenhardt, who had forty victories in the spring of 1917 and who later went on to score sixteen more; Karl Allmenroeder and Karl Schaefer, with thirty victories each; Kurt Wolff, with twenty-seven at the time of the Battle of Arras; Otto Bernert with twenty-six; and many others who were to be numbered among the German Flying Corps' fifty top-scorers before the end of the war.

In accordance with the German policy of concentrating their

10

best pilots into single crack units, most of the above-named men served with von Richthofen's *Jagdstaffel* 11. A *Jagdstaffel*, abbreviated to *Jasta*, usually consisted of twelve or fourteen aircraft, although later this was increased to twenty-one. In June 1917 *Jastas* 4, 6, 10 and 11 were merged into a single *Jagdgeschwader* (Fighter Wing) under Richthofen's command. Although patrols were still flown at *Jasta* strength, Richthofen could, in response to an increase in Allied air activity, concentrate a large number of fighter aircraft in any particular sector of the front. Moreover, the *Jagdgeschwader* was highly mobile and could be switched quickly from one part of the front to another in support of ground operations.

The principal German fighter aircraft in the spring of 1917 was the Albatros DIII, which had first been issued to *Jasta* 11 in January of that year. Powered by a Mercedes DIII engine, it had a maximum speed of 108 mph and carried an armament of twin synchronized 7.92 Spandau machine-guns. By April 1917 all thirty-seven *Jastas* at the front were equipped with either the DIII or the earlier Albatros DII.

However, the most widely used of all the Albatros fighters was the DV, which made its appearance in mid-1917. It was not a great improvement over the excellent DIII, but it was produced in large numbers, over 1,500 serving with the *Jastas* on the Western Front alone.

Later in the year, starting in August, some *Jastas* also began to receive the Pfalz DIII, which like the Albatros was powered by a Mercedes engine and featured twin Spandau machine-guns. However, even at its peak the Pfalz fully equipped only about a dozen units, and for some reason German pilots seem to have been prejudiced against it; this attitude is hard to understand, because the Pfalz was a sturdy machine, capable of absorbing a great deal of battle damage, and it could be dived harder and faster than the Albatros.

The other new German fighter type introduced in 1917 was the Fokker DrI Triplane. Its design was inspired by the Sopwith Triplane, an excellent and highly manoeuvrable fighter which served with Nos 1, 8, 9, 10, 11 and 12 Squadrons of the Royal Naval Air Service (RNAS) on the Western Front during most of 1917. The Fokker Triplane was never used in very large numbers, but it registered astonishing successes in the hands of leading German aces such as von Richthofen and Voss.

To counter the threat posed by the *Jagdgeschwader* in the summer of 1917, the RFC was forced to adopt a similar policy of concentrating its best fighter squadrons and pilots in opposition to von Richthofen wherever his squadrons appeared. These elite RFC units were the cradle of the leading British fighter aces. No 56 Squadron, for example, in addition to Albert Ball, numbered among its ranks such famous fighter pilots as Captain James McCudden, Lieutenant Rhys-Davids, Captain Brunwin-Hales with twenty-seven victories and Captain Henry Burden with twenty-two; then there was Captain W. A. (Billy) Bishop of No 60 Squadron (and later of No 85), a Canadian who was to survive the war as the second-ranking RFC fighter ace with seventy-two victories, being narrowly beaten to the top by Major Mick Mannock, who had a score of at least seventy-four. Mannock flew with No 40 Squadron, as did two other leading fighter aces: Captain G. E. H. McElroy, a Canadian with a score of forty-six, and Major Roderic Dallas, a New Zealander, with thirty-nine.

In fact, the formation of large, concentrated fighter groups had been pioneered by the French during the Battle of the Somme in the summer of 1916, when the Cachy Group (so-called after its operational base near Amiens) came into existence under the command of Captain Brocard of N3 *Cigognes*. (To avoid confusion, it should be pointed out that the French squadrons bore the initial letter of the aircraft type they were flying; the *Cigognes* were using Nieuports at the time, and later, when they converted to SPADs, their designation was changed to SPA 3.) The Cachy Group comprised N3, with Guynemer as its leading pilot, and Captain Féquant's N65, which included Charles Nungesser.

At the end of 1916 the French Aéronautique Militaire possessed three *Groupes de Combat*: GC 11 under Commandant Le Révérend, GC 12 under Commandant Brocard, and GC 13 under Commandant Féquant. Eleven more would be formed before the end of hostilities. Each *Groupe* comprised four *Escadrilles*, each with fifteen aircraft and fifteen pilots. The *Groupes de Combat* came under the orders of the French army commanders and, like their Royal Flying Corps counter-parts, had the task of establishing air superiority and protecting observation aircraft. In 1917, mixed units of fighters and bombers were employed in carrying out offensive operations.

The aircraft on which most of the French aces cut their teeth was the Nieuport 11C-1 *Bébé*, which entered service in the summer of 1915 and which was also used in some numbers by the RFC and RNAS. It was this little aircraft which helped to redress the balance of power following the appearance over the Western Front of the Fokker E.III Monoplane, with its syn-chronized machine-gun firing through the propeller. The *Bébé* was followed into service, in May 1916, by the Nieuport 17C-1, which equipped *Escadrilles* N3, N38, N55, N57, N65 and N103. It also served with eight RNAS and five RFC squadrons.

In the autumn of 1916 many *Escadrilles* began to re-equip with a new fighter type, the SPAD VII (the initial letters stand for *Société Pour l'Aviation et ses Derivées*). Although less manoeuvrable than the Nieuport types, the SPAD VII was a strong, stable gun platform with a top speed of 119 mph and an excellent rate of climb. The SPAD VII was also used by the RFC and RNAS, and filled a crucial gap at a time when many units were still equipped with ageing and vulnerable aircraft.

In May 1917, however, the French *Escadrilles de Chasse* began to standardize on a new type, the SPAD XIII. Like its predecessor, it was an excellent gun platform and was also extremely strong, although it was tricky to fly at low speeds. Powered by a Hispano-Suiza 8Ba engine and armed with two forward-firing Vickers guns, it had a maximum speed of nearly 140 mph – quite exceptional for that time – and could climb to 22,000 feet. The SPAD XIII subsequently equipped more than eighty *Escadrilles*.

Such, in broad outline, was the state of air power on both sides of the front – discounting bomber and observation types for the moment – when the British opened a new offensive in Flanders in June 1917, the main effort taking place in the Messines sector. The attack was supported by eighteen RFC squadrons with a total of 300 aircraft, about one-third of them single-seat fighters. On the first day of the offensive, 7 June, Captain W. A. Bishop of No 60 Squadron was awarded the Victoria Cross for destroying four out of seven enemy aircraft in a daring single-handed attack on an airfield near Cambrai. He was flying a Nieuport 17.

By the end of the month the RFC's reserves were sadly depleted. The situation was further aggravated by the withdrawal on 21 June of two of its best fighter squadrons, Nos 56 and 66, for home defence. This also helped to delay the re-equipment of RFC units in France with new aircraft, notably the Sopwith Camel.

For the RFC crews, stretched to their utmost during July, it was some consolation to know that von Richthofen was out of action for a time. On 6 July, forty fighters of the Richthofen *Jagdgeschwader* had attacked six FE2ds of No 20 Squadron, escorted by four Sopwith Triplanes of No 10 Squadron RNAS; two FEs were shot down, but an observer in another – 2nd Lieutenant A. E. Woodbridge – got in a good burst at Richthofen's red Albatros and sent it down to make a forced landing. Richthofen was wounded in the head.

The days before the third battle of Ypres, which opened on 31 July, were marked by intense air activity on both sides. At this time the combined strength of the RFC, RNAS, l'Aéronautique Militaire and the small Belgian Air Corps on the Western Front was 852 aircraft, of which 360 were fighters; the German strength was 600 machines, of which 200 were fighters.

To bolster the Allied fighter strength in Flanders, two French *Escadrilles* – including the *Cigognes* – were sent to Dunkirk from the Lorraine sector. Charles Nungesser, having experienced engine trouble, was flying alone a few hours behind the rest when he was suddenly attacked by a British aircraft near Arras and took fifteen bullets through his Nieuport. Convinced that the attacking aircraft was a captured one, flown by a German crew, he engaged it and shot it down, landing nearby to inspect the wreck. The pilot was dead, and Nungesser, finding some identity documents on the body, discovered to his dismay that the man who had tried to kill him was in fact an RFC pilot – a very inexperienced one, as a subsequent enquiry established.

The air offensive that preceded the battle opened on 11 July, and on the first day fourteen German aircraft were destroyed for the loss of nine British. A few days later von Richthofen was back in action, his head still in bandages, and a series of

14

massive dogfights took place between his *Jagdgeschwader* and Allied fighter formations. On the twenty-sixth, no fewer than ninety-four single-seat fighters fought one another at altitudes varying between 5,000 and 7,000 feet over Polygon Wood, and the following evening thirty Albatros fighters attacked eight FE2ds over the same area. It was a trap; no sooner had the German fighters come down to intercept than they were attacked by fifty-nine SE5s and Sopwith Triplanes. Nine enemy aircraft were destroyed for the loss of one SE5.

The *Cigognes* had seldom encountered pilots of the calibre of those who made up the Richthofen *Jagdgeschwader* in the skies of Lorraine, where they had helped to defend the embattled fortress of Verdun, and they found Flanders a tough battleground. Georges Madon had an incredible escape when, flying a new SPAD XIII with which the *Escadrille* was equipping, he collided with an enemy two-seater. With his upper wing torn completely away, he spun out of control through a terrifying 10,000 feet. Literally at the last moment his aircraft miraculously righted itself before crash-landing in the Allied lines, breaking itself into pièces. His only injury was a broken finger.

Another ace, Lieutenant Albert Deullin, was not so lucky. During a fight with an enemy monoplane, he took two bullets in the region of his kidneys and crash-landed, gravely wounded. He survived to fly and fight again in 1918. Alfred Heurtaux, attacking a two-seater near Ypres, was hit in the thigh. Fainting through loss of blood, he went into a spin and recovered just in time to right his aircraft. He spotted a field dead ahead and went down to land on it; it turned out to be an RFC aerodrome, and the British whisked him off to hospital. Among the other French pilots, Lieutenant Chaput crashed and was injured, while the ace of aces, Guynemer, was wounded and hospitalized. Nungesser, Fonck and Jean Navarre fought on, but it was an increasingly grim business.

One day in July, Nungesser made a lone diving attack on six German scouts over Houthulst Forest. He made a single pass, shooting down two of them and then using his superior speed to get away. The others made off eastwards under the command of a young pilot who, after flying two-seater reconnaissance missions with a unit known as *Abteilung* 5, had recently transferred to single-seaters with *Jasta* 27. His name was Hermann Goering.

When the ground offensive began on 31 July much of the Allied effort was switched to attacks on enemy airfields and infantry columns with light bombs as well as machine-guns. For the first time in the war, large-scale ground attack operations were carried out by the fighter units, with devastating effect on the closely packed enemy troops and supply columns. However, it was dangerous work, and casualties from ground fire were heavy. Moreover, the terrain was by no means in the favour of any pilot who had to make a forced landing. 'In front of us,' wrote René Fonck, 'there was nothing but miles and miles of spongy ground, where water crept stealthily into the tiniest hole. The whole area was a vast quagmire that could swallow up an object as big as a tank without trace.'

By September 1917, the Allied fighter squadrons in Flanders had succeeded, for the time being, in establishing a measure of air superiority. On 25 September, the RFC's fighter squadrons claimed nineteen victories for the loss of only one British aircraft. No 56 Squadron, which had returned to France in July after a brief stay in England, continued to be in the forefront of the battle; by the end of September its score of enemy aircraft destroyed had risen to 200. This figure was matched, on 9 October, by No 1 Squadron, now equipped with Sopwith Camels.

Then, just as the Allies were starting to gain the upper hand in the air, there came a new and alarming development that was to have an enormous bearing on the conduct of the entire war. In November 1917 the revolutionary Bolshevik regime in Russia signed an armistice with the Germans. This meant that the hundreds of thousands of German troops, together with large numbers of guns and aircraft, which had been tied down in the war with Tsarist Russia could now be released for service on the Western Front. There was every possibility that the Germans would attempt a final massive offensive designed to smash the Allied armies once and for all in the early part of 1918, before American forces began to arrive on the Continent in large numbers.

In the last weeks of 1917, with substantial enemy troop

movements from east to west already apparent, air reconnaissance became of paramount importance to the Allies. The observation squadrons embarked on an intense period of flying, and suffered heavy losses in the process. One such was No 10 Squadron which, equipped with Armstrong Whitworth F.K.8s, was based at Abeele, in Belgium; its tasks were corps reconnaissance, line patrol and night bombing, all of which it carried out successfully but unspectacularly during this period. During the night of 30/31 October, for example, this squadron dropped thirty-nine 20-lb Cooper bombs on enemy communications at Henin Lietard and Billy Montigny; the next day, in co-operation with a daylight attack by the 46th Infantry Division, the F.K.8s dropped three 112-lb high explosive, sixty-three 20-lb high explosive and twenty 40-lb phosphorus bombs in the front and on the flanks of the enemy positions. To round off the attack, the pilots and observers also fired 1,200 rounds into enemy communications trenches.

Designed by Frederick Koolhoven, the F.K.8 – known as the 'Big Ack' by its crews – equipped Nos 2, 8, 10, 35 and 82 Squadrons on the Western Front in late 1917. Its 160 hp Beardmore engine gave it a top speed of around 90 mph and it carried an armament of one synchronized Vickers gun, operated by the pilot, and a Lewis gun in the rear cockpit. Although heavy on the controls, especially the ailerons and elevators, it was well built and robust, could absorb a lot of battle damage and was well liked by its crews. Major K. D. P. Murray, No 10 Squadron's commanding officer, said of it:

'The big A-W was slow, but my pilots liked it for the particular job they had to do, and never regarded themselves as "cold meat". Owing to the nature of their work, they were rarely in a position to attack, but when attacked, as they were frequently enough, they gave a good enough account of themselves.'

One of No 10 Squadron's crews who definitely gave a good account of themselves were Captain John Pattern and Lieutenant Leycester, who took off together on a photo-reconnaissance sortie on 29 November 1917. Pattern himself, shortly before his death (he was then in his nineties), told the story to the author:

17

'I was due to go home on leave the following day, and when you had been warned for leave you weren't supposed to fly. But after several days of fog and rain the weather had finally cleared and there were reports of large enemy troop movements south of Passchendaele, so as the Squadron's most experienced pilot I was detailed to go out and get the photographs that were urgently needed. It wasn't that I was a particularly good pilot; it was just that most of the others were dead. On average, a crew doing our sort of job, flying straight and level over the enemy lines, could expect to last three weeks before being shot down. Some of us, myself included, were lucky; I had been shot down only a week before, and had walked out of the wreck with only a few scratches. That was one of the good points about the big A-W: it was so strongly built that crews could often walk away from the most horrendous crashes.'

On that November morning, Pattern and Leycester – it was their seventh mission together – took off from Abeele and climbed to 5,000 feet, heading towards Ypres and the front line. Unknown to them, some thirty miles away another pilot was also taking off from an airfield near Lille. He was Lieutenant Erwin Boehme, a *Staffel* commander in the Richthofen *Jagdgeschwader*.

This was a big day in Boehme's life. In a few hours' time he was due to receive Germany's highest award for gallantry – the *Ordre Pour le Mérite* or 'Blue Max' as it was nicknamed – from the hands of the Kaiser himself. The medal was Boehme's reward for shooting down twenty-four British and French aircraft, but to him its significance was much greater. It would help to remove a burden of guilt he had carried for a year now, since October 1916.

Together with his *Staffel* commander, Oswald Boelcke – the most famous German air ace of that time – he had been involved in a dogfight with some British aircraft. Boehme had made a slight error of judgement. His wingtip had touched Boelcke's and the ace's aircraft had gone down, breaking up as it fell. Boelcke had been killed instantly. Desolate, Boehme had gone to his tent on landing and taken out his revolver, intent on committing suicide, but had been prevented by von Richthofen. Now, in November 1917, Boehme commanded Boelcke's old unit, *Jagdstaffel* 2.

Boehme headed for the front line, accompanied by five more Albatros Scouts, intent on claiming one more victim before he received his decoration. That victim should have been John Pattern, whose F.K.8 was crossing the front line just north of Westhoek. Pattern takes up the story:

'About a quarter of a mile on the enemy side of the lines, I turned south-east and Leycester started to work his cameras. The anti-aircraft fire, which had been intense, had not stopped, but I didn't take much notice. I should have known better; it was a sure sign that enemy fighters were in the vicinity. Suddenly, I heard the clatter of Leycester's machine-gun above the roar of the engine. I looked round to see what he was shooting at, and nearly had a heart attack. Slanting down from above, getting nicely into position thirty yards behind my tail, was an Albatros.

'I immediately heaved the old A-W round in a split-arse turn, tighter I think than I had ever turned before. I felt a flash of panic as I lost sight of the Hun, but Leycester must have been able to see him all right as he kept on firing. My sudden turn had done the trick. The Albatros overshot and suddenly appeared right in front of me. Because of the relative motion of our two aircraft, he seemed to hang motionless, suspended in mid-air. I could see the pilot's face as he looked back at me.

'I sent a two-second burst of Vickers fire into him. His aircraft seemed to flutter, then slid out of sight below my starboard wing. I was pretty certain that I had hit his petrol tank. Behind me, Leycester was still blazing away. He was using tracer, and it may have been one of his bullets that ignited the petrol pouring from the Hun's ruptured tank. When I caught sight of the Albatros again, it was burning like a torch and side-slipping towards the ground, trailing a streamer of smoke. For an instant I saw the German pilot, looking down over the side of the cockpit. Then the smoke and flames enveloped him.

'I pushed the A-W's nose down and headed flat out for home, aware that the other Hun scouts were coming down fast after me. They would probably have got me, too, if some friendly fighters had not come along just in time and driven them away. To say that I was relieved would be the understatement of the century.

'In due course I learned the name of the man I had shot down, but I didn't take much notice at the time. It was not until fifty years later that I came across the full story of Erwin Boehme's career in some

19

book or other. My first reaction was that if I had known who he was at the time he attacked me, I would have shoved the A-W's nose down and landed in the nearest available field. But then, maybe I wouldn't have. Who knows?

'All I do know is how lucky Leycester and I were, on that day over Flanders.'

CHAPTER TWO

The year 1918 began dismally for the Allies. The French Army, its spring offensive of 1917 having petered out amid tragic and bloody loss, had been in little fit state to mount any major offensive during the remainder of the year except at Verdun, where it had registered some success in the summer; moreover, its High Command had been rocked to the foundations by widespread mutinies among its embittered soldiers. The British had suffered fearful losses in men and material in the bitter and protracted third battle of Ypres, while on the southern front the Italians had been utterly crushed at Caporetto. Then, to crown it all, had come the ruthless armistice terms imposed upon the Russians by the Germans at Brest-Litovsk.

America was in the war and was mobilizing swiftly, but the US First Army Corps, comprising the 1st, 2nd, 26th and 42nd Divisions, was still in the process of formation; its men were untrained and it would be months before they were ready to go into the line. The German Chief of Staff, 53-year-old General Erich Ludendorff, knew this perfectly well. By the spring of 1918, before the Americans entered the battle, he would have 200 divisions, many of the latter weak and under strength. Spring would be the time to strike, to force the British back into the sea, to seize the Channel ports and bring about the rapid disintegration of the Franco-Belgian armies.

In the early weeks of 1918 the Americans were even more ill-fitted to contribute to the air war in France than they were to take part in the land campaign. In 1917, American military air power, such as it was, was embodied in the Aviation Section of the US Signal Corps; its inventory of less than 300 aircraft did not include a single combat machine. Following America's entry into the war, and a resulting massive increase in the budget available to expand the country's military aviation, the US Army sent Colonel Raynal Bolling to Europe for a first-hand look at the type of equipment that would be needed by the American air units joining the Allied forces. Bolling found American volunteer pilots flying British and French aircraft that were already far superior to anything the embryo American aviation industry could design and produce in the limited time available, and so it was decided that the Americans would concentrate on building training and reconnaissance aircraft while their future combat pilots flew Nieuports and SPADs.

The nucleus of those combat pilots, and a highly experienced one at that, already existed. American volunteers had been serving with the Aéronautique Militaire since 1915, having arrived via the French Foreign Legion, which had granted them French citizenship for the duration of their military service and so neatly avoided any possible political complications. In the autumn of 1915, the idea of banding all the Americans together in one squadron had been nurtured by Edmund L. Gros, a doctor of medicine who had already helped to form an American Ambulance Service in France during the early months of the war. The original idea was not that of Gros, but of a young pilot named Norman Prince, of Pride's Crossing in Massachusetts, who came to Paris, teamed up with the doctor and started a recruiting campaign to comb the Foreign Legion, the Ambulance Service and the French forces in search of Americans who might be willing to volunteer for flying duties. As soon as a likely candidate was located, and showed willing, Gros had him transferred to the Aéronautique Militaire for training; this step was accomplished with the help of Jarousse de Silac, a senior member of the French War Ministry, who believed that it was only a matter of time before America entered the war on the Allied side anyway.

As soon as the American airmen completed their training they were posted to various air units for operational service, while Gros and his colleagues worked hard behind the scenes to obtain official approval for the formation of an American squadron. The word spread quickly and more volunteers began to arrive from the United States, some of them having already tried to join the RFC. In the spring of 1916 they were all either operational or under training in France, awaiting the call from Gros and Prince.

It came on 17 April 1916. On that day the *Escadrille Américaine* – known officially as *Escadrille* N124 – was formed around a nucleus of seven pilots, with Norman Prince at their head. During the next few days seven more arrived, having been detached from their respective French units. Among them was Raoul Lufbery, who had been one of the first to enlist in 1915.

The *Escadrille*, which was equipped with Nieuport Scouts, moved up to Bar-le-Duc, in the Verdun sector, and its pilots – many of whom had already acquired considerable experience with the French – soon began to distinguish themselves. The first to score was Lieutenant Kiffin Rockwell, who shot down a two-seater on 18 May, and who destroyed two more enemy aircraft before the end of the year. Norman Prince claimed five victories before he was killed in a flying accident in October, while Lieutenants Bert Hall and Bill Thaw got two and one respectively. But the rising star of the *Escadrille* was a man who had once been told by his French flying instructors that he was not sufficiently competent to fly fighter aircraft: Raoul Lufbery, who claimed six enemy aircraft before the close of 1916.

Late in 1916 the *Escadrille* moved to the Somme sector. By this time its fighting prowess was so well established that the German Government lodged a protest with the United States against the unit's existence, claiming that the word '*Américaine*' in its title was a violation of US neutrality. The French Government accordingly decided to change the title to the *Escadrille Lafayette*, the name recalling the French soldier and nobleman who had fought for the Americans in the War of Independence.

By the end of 1917 the score of the *Escadrille Lafayette* stood at forty-two enemy aircraft destroyed. The leading scorer was Raoul Lufbery, with sixteen, followed by Lieutenants Bill Thaw and de Laage – the latter a Frenchman – with four each. In January 1918 Lufbery was commissioned into the American Air Service with the rank of major, and expected to receive orders to form an American fighter squadron. Instead, to his disgust, he was sent to a training school at Issoudun, where recruits to the Air Service were knocked into shape before starting their flying courses. It was to be three months before he returned to operational flying.

Meanwhile, a strange and ominous silence hung over the

23

snow-shrouded wasteland of Flanders during the early days of 1918. One of the first sorties flown by the Allies was carried out early on New Year's Day by three RE8 reconnaissance aircraft of No 3 Squadron, Australian Flying Corps, which photographed the entire Australian Corps' front in the Messines sector; the reconnaissances showed signs of heavy transport at the rear of the German lines, and revealed that ammunition dumps were increasing and more gun positions being built.

No 3 (Australian) Squadron, which had arrived in Flanders in September 1917, had seen some hard fighting during the previous weeks. Flying from Savy, halfway between St Pol and Arras, it was attached to No 1 (Corps) Wing RFC and ordered to act as support squadron to the RFC squadrons on duty with the two Army Corps in the line: No 5 Squadron RFC, with the Canadian Corps, and No 16 Squadron RFC with XIII Corps. All three squadrons were equipped with the Royal Aircraft Factory RE8, the most widely used British two-seater on the Western Front. Like the F.K.8, the RE8 carried an armament of one forward-firing Vickers gun with a Lewis gun in the observer's cockpit. It was powered by an R.A.F.4a engine, which gave it a top speed of around 102 mph. It was a good deal less durable than its Armstrong Whitworth counterpart, and the Germans found it a lot easier to shoot down.

Nevertheless, the RE8 – nicknamed 'Harry Tate' – could give a good account of itself, as was shown on the afternoon of 17 December 1917 when an aircraft of No 3 (Australian) Squadron, ranging for an eight-inch howitzer battery, was attacked by six Albatros DV scouts. Although hard pressed, the RE's pilot, Lieutenant J. L. M. Sandy, shot down one Albatros; its wounded pilot made a forced landing in the Australian lines and was taken prisoner. Then another RE8 came up and its pilot and observer joined Sandy in engaging the enemy. The two REs fought the five Albatros for nearly ten minutes, until the Germans saw a third RE8 approaching and broke off the engagement.

The pilot of the second RE8, Lieutenant E. J. Jones, flew close to Sandy's aircraft, which was cruising normally, and thought that its pilot and observer, Sergeant H. F. Hughes, were uninjured and that they were continuing their sortie, so he flew back to base to re-arm. The next day, No 3 Squadron received a telegram to say that the bodies of Sandy and Hughes had been found in their wrecked aircraft near St Pol. An examination showed that a bullet had passed through the observer and lodged in the base of the pilot's skull. The aircraft had flown itself in wide left-hand circles until it ran out of fuel, and then crashed about fifty miles south-west of the battle area. Sandy was recommended for an immediate award of the Military Cross and Hughes for the Distinguished Conduct Medal.

Another German pilot who fell victim to an RE8 was Lieutenant Max Mueller, one of *Jasta* Boelcke's leading pilots. On 29 November 1917, the day Erwin Boehme was shot down, Mueller scored the *Jasta*'s 179th victory and then became a flight commander under the new *Staffelführer*, Lieutenant Walter von Bülow. On 16 December he scored his thirty-eighth and final victory, shooting down a Sopwith Camel west of Passchendaele.

Von Bülow was killed on 6 January 1918, and Mueller was appointed *Staffelführer* in his place. On 8 January, Mueller visited the *Jagdstaffelschule* at Valenciennes and delivered a lecture to a class of student pilots on the best methods of shooting down an RE8. The next day he was back with his *Jasta* at Marke, taking off at the head of six more Albatros DVs to put his theories into practice. Near Passchendaele, he sighted an RE8 and led his pilots down for a formation attack. Captain G. Zimmer, the pilot of the RE8 – which belonged to No 21 Squadron RFC, said by many to be the finest artillery observation squadron on the Western Front – saw the seven Albatros coming down on him and turned hard, enabling his observer, 2nd Lieutenant H. Somerville, to put a good burst into the leading Albatros at close range. The Albatros, after firing one burst at the RE8, suddenly veered away and began to glide with its engine stopped. Then it burst into flames and dropped away out of control.

A few thousand feet lower down, Max Mueller jumped from the cockpit of his blazing aircraft and plummeted to his death near the ruined town of Moorslede. The other German pilots, horrified, broke off their attack on the RE8, which escaped over the front line.

On 19 January, ten days after Mueller's death, the *Cigognes* parted company with the Flanders front and returned to Verdun, where they soon made their presence felt. They were now commanded by Commandant Hormant, who had replaced Brocard. On the day of their return, Hormant proposed an offensive patrol over enemy territory; René Fonck, Captain Pierre d'Harcourt and another pilot named Fontaine volunteered. Over the front line they encountered a superior formation of enemy aircraft, which they attacked. In the middle of the fight, Fonck noticed that Fontaine was in difficulty, his engine having apparently failed, and was being harassed by two German machines. Fonck quickly shot down his own adversary, then dived on Fontaine's attackers. Within seconds one of them, too, was spinning down in flames. The other fled and Fontaine made a safe emergency landing.

On 27 January, taking advantage of a break in the increasingly poor weather, Captain Georges Madon shot down his twenty-first victim, and two days later shot down a two-seater which had strayed too far inside French territory for its own safety. Another was destroyed by Charles Nungesser. On 3 February Madon shot down two more, bringing his score to twenty-four, and destroyed another a few days later after a hectic fight against six enemy scouts. Nungesser, still in top place, was working hard to gain his thirty-second victory, but so far success was eluding him. Among the talented pilots of the *Cigognes*, the race to be 'ace of aces' was on again.

Meanwhile, in London, steps were being taken that were to transform the whole conduct of the air war. On 17 August 1917, a committee presided over by Lieutenant General Jan Smuts had presented a report on air organization to the War Cabinet. It recommended the formation of an Air Ministry 'to control and administer all matters in connection with air warfare of every kind and that the new Ministry should proceed to work out the arrangements for the amalgamation of the two Services and for the legal constitution and discipline of the new Service.' It went on to point out that 'The day may not be far off when aerial operations with their devastation of enemy lands and destruction of industrial and populous centres on a vast scale may become the principal operations of war, to which the older forms of military and naval operations may become secondary and subordinate.'

26

This remarkably far-sighted report resulted in the creation of an Air Ministry on 2 January 1918, although its birth was not accomplished without a considerable amount of inter-Service wrangling. On the following day the first Air Council was formed, with Lord Rothermere as the first Secretary of State for Air. The Chief of the Air Staff was Major General Sir Hugh Trenchard, who was succeeded as General Officer Commanding the Royal Flying Corps in France by Major General J. M. Salmond on 18 January. The first moves had been made towards the creation of the Royal Air Force, the first independent force of its kind in the world.

This same period, the winter of 1917–18, also saw a reorganization of Britain's air defences. The day of the large-scale Zeppelin raids on Britain was over, hampered by the weather and lack of navigational skills from the beginning, and finally crippled by the growing proficiency of the RFC's night-fighter crews and the anti-aircraft defences. But from the summer of 1917 a much greater threat emerged with the beginning of sustained attacks on British targets by the Gotha bombers of *Kagohl* 3 (the unit's designation being an abbreviation of *Kampfgeschwader der Obersten Heeresleitung*) of German High Command Bomber Wing.

Powered by a pair of 260 hp Mercedes DIVa liquid-cooled in-line engines, the Gotha GIV could carry a typical bomb load of six 110-lb bombs. Its maximum speed was about 85 mph, which even so was faster than some of the fighter aircraft sent up to intercept it, and its attack altitude of 16,000 feet made it a difficult target, unless defensive fighters had ample warning of its approach. The first attack on the British mainland, mounted by twenty-three Gothas in daylight on 25 May 1917, killed 95 civilians and injured 195 in Folkestone. More than seventy home defence aircraft were sent up to intercept, but the only ones to make contact were flown by two ferry pilots. Several Gothas were destroyed in subsequent raids, but these mostly fell to anti-aircraft fire or failed to regain their base because of adverse weather. The few home defence aircraft that did get close enough to intercept were usually beaten off by the Gotha's substantial defensive armament of three Spandau machine-guns.

In September 1917 the Gothas switched to night attacks, and

they were now joined by an even more formidable bomber: the Zeppelin (Staaken) R Type, known as the *Riesenflugzeug* (giant aircraft). This monster was capable of carrying a 2,200-lb bomb at 14,000 feet at 80 mph under the power of its four 260 hp Mercedes engines; moreover it was defended by five machine-guns, which made it a much tougher target than the Gotha. Only a small number of R Types were built, but they presented an immense threat to British targets. To meet this threat, the War Office implemented a new defence scheme whereby anti-aircraft guns and patrolling aircraft were allocated separate operating zones. In addition, balloons trailing steel cable 'curtains' floated in barriers up to 8,000 feet, theoretically forcing any attacking aircraft to fly above that height to a level where fighters would be patrolling.

The first German bombing raid of 1918 was mounted on the night of 28/29 January, when thirteen Gothas and two Giants were despatched to attack London. In the event seven Gothas and one Giant succeeded in doing so, killing 67 civilians, injuring another 166, and causing damage of nearly £190,000. The raid was thwarted to some degree by fog, as far as the Gothas were concerned, while one of the Giants had engine trouble and was forced to turn back, having jettisoned its bombs into the sea off Ostende.

Crossing the English coast at intervals from 8.00 pm between Harwich and the North Foreland, three Gothas bombed London and the remaining four attacked Ramsgate, Margate, Sheerness and Sandwich. The Giant also reached London just after midnight, and one of its two 660-lb bombs caused the worst single bombing incident of the war when it hit the Odhams Press building in Long Acre, killing 38 people and injuring 85.

One of the Gothas involved in the London attack, crewed by Lieutenant Friedrich von Thomsen (navigator and commander) and Sergeants Karl Ziegler (pilot) and Walther Heiden, dropped its bombs on Hampstead at 9.45 pm and was then tracked by searchlights as it flew over north-east London. The beams attracted the attention of two patrolling Sopwith Camel pilots of No 44 Squadron from Hainault – Captain George Hackwill and Lieutenant Charles Banks – who at once gave chase and independently picked up the glow from the Gotha's exhausts as it passed over Romford at 10,000 feet. Banks was flying a Camel with an unconventional armament; in addition to its normal pair of Vickers guns it also carried a Lewis, mounted on the upper wing centre section and using the new RTS ammunition. Designed by Richard Threlfall and Son, this combined explosive and incendiary qualities.

It was Banks who attacked first, closing from the left to about thirty yards beneath the Gotha and opening fire with all three guns. Hackwill meanwhile closed in from the right and also opened fire, effectively boxing in the German bomber and presenting an impossible situation to its gunner, whose field of fire was restricted. After ten minutes or so the Gotha caught fire and dived into the ground near Wickford, where it exploded. It would almost certainly have crashed anyway, even if it had not caught fire, for a subsequent examination of the crew's bodies revealed that the pilot had been shot through the neck. Hackwill and Banks were each awarded the Military Cross for their exploit.

Other Gothas were also attacked that night, briefly and without result, by pilots of Nos 39, 50, 61 and 78 Squadrons RFC, and by a Sopwith 1½-Strutter of the RNAS from Dover.

An hour after the last Gotha had cleared the coast, the *Riesenflugzeug* was over Sudbury, having made landfall over Hollesley Bay, east of Ipswich, and was droning towards London via a somewhat tortuous route. By this time, at least forty-four fighters were searching for it. It was sighted by two of them, from an unidentified squadron, not long after crossing the coast, but they lost contact with it and it was next sighted by the crew of a No 39 Squadron Bristol Fighter at about 11.00 pm near Harlow. The pilot of the Bristol, Lieutenant John Goodyear, positioned himself behind the Giant and fired a long burst from his Vickers, but was then hurled aside by the slipstream; this Giant, an R.12, was fitted with six coupled engines driving three propellers, and the wash they created was enormous.

He tried again, and the same thing happened. On the third attempt, with the Bristol now running through heavy defensive fire, he tried to position underneath the Giant so that his gunner, 1st Air Mechanic W. T. Merchant, could bring fire from his Lewis gun to bear. At that moment a burst of fire from one of the German gunners shattered the Bristol's petrol tank and wounded Merchant slightly in the arm. A few moments later the engine stopped and Goodyear glided down to make a faultless engine-off landing at North Weald, whose flarepath he had seen in the distance.

Shortly after it had released its bombs over London, the Giant was picked up east of Woolwich by a Sopwith Camel of No 44 Squadron flown by Lieutenant Bob Hall, a South African. Hall followed it as far as Foulness, cursing in helpless frustration all the way because he could not get his guns to work. The Giant got clean away.

The anti-aircraft barrage scored one success that night, but unfortunately its victim was a Camel of No 78 Squadron flown by 2nd Lieutenant Idris Davies, whose engine was stopped by a near shell burst at 11,000 feet over Woolwich. Davies tried to glide back to Sutton's Farm, but he hit telegraph wires near the Hornchurch signal box and was catapulted out of the cockpit. He fell between the railway lines, amazingly without injury, but the Camel was a complete loss. Forty minutes later Davies was sitting in another Camel, ready to take off if need be. Mostly, the anti-aircraft gunners co-operated very well with the RFC, and held their fire when friendly fighters were known to be overhead.

The following night witnessed the most remarkable night battle of the First World War, when three Giants out of four despatched attacked southern England. The fourth, having developed engine trouble over the Channel, bombed fortifications near Gravelines before returning to its base, while the others crossed the English coast between Southend and The Naze. Of these, one, the R.26, developed engine trouble soon after crossing the coast and began losing height, so its crew jettisoned the bomb load and limped back across the Channel on two engines, eventually landing at Ostende.

A second Giant, the R.39, came inland via the Blackwater estuary just after 10.00 pm, and ten minutes later it was sighted by Captain Arthur Dennis of No 37 Squadron, who was flying a BE12b. The latter, developed from the older BE2c, had enjoyed some success in the night-fighting role, one of No 37 Squadron's aircraft having shot down Zeppelin L48 in June 1917. It was armed with a single Lewis gun, mounted on the port side of the cockpit and synchronized to fire through the propeller. Dennis opened fire from close range, braving fire from two of the Giant's machine-guns, and scored hits on the bomber's fuselage before drawing off to change his ammunition drum. On the second approach, however, he was buffeted by the Giant's slipstream, and on recovery found that he had lost contact with the target.

The R.39 approached London from the north-west at 11,000 feet and was next sighted by Bob Hall of No 44 Squadron, who pursued it until it became lost in the haze near Roehampton. Once again, Hall's guns gave trouble and he had no opportunity to open fire. Meanwhile, the Giant had dropped its bombs on residential areas between Acton and Richmond Park, the crew having apparently mistaken Hammersmith Bridge for Tower Bridge, which was several miles to the east. South of the Thames, the R.39 was attacked briefly and with no visible result by Captain F. L. Luxmoore of No 78 Squadron, flying a Sopwith Camel. He fired fifty rounds on his first pass, but as he made a second firing run one of his bullets struck the Camel's propeller and the brilliant tracer element flew back into his face, temporarily blinding him. By the time his night vision was restored, the bomber had vanished.

Shortly after this the R.39, now down to 9,500 feet and travelling very fast, was located by Captain G. H. Hackwill of No 44 Squadron, who was also flying a Camel. Hackwill gave chase and fired 600 rounds from long range before shortage of fuel compelled him to break off. The Giant was last seen as it crossed the coast near Hythe by 2nd Lieutenants F. V. Bryant and V. H. Newton, the crew of an Armstrong Whitworth F.K.8 of No 50 Squadron. They too gave chase, but lost the bomber in haze.

The third Giant, the R.25, crossed the coast near Foulness at 10.50 pm and was almost immediately attacked by 2nd Lieutenant F. R. Kitton of No 37 Squadron, flying a BE2e. Diving his aircraft at a shuddering 100 mph, he got under the Giant's tail and fired a complete drum of ammunition at it, observing several hits, but lost the bomber while he was busy rearming. The R.25 was next attacked by Bob Hall of No 44 Squadron at 11.15 pm over Benfleet, but his guns kept on jamming as he pursued it. He was joined by 2nd Lieutenant H. A. Edwardes, also of No 44 Squadron, who fired three long bursts before his guns also jammed.

By this time the R.25 was taking violent evasive action. The battle had now attracted three more Camels, all from No 44 Squadron; the first on the scene was 2nd Lieutenant T. M. O'Neill, who fired 300 rounds before his guns jammed too. Next came the squadron commander, Major Murlis Green, who was flying a Camel equipped with two Lewis guns using RTS ammunition. He had already made one run, only to break away when he almost flew into O'Neill's fire. Now he closed in again to be greeted by the full attention of the Giant's rear gunner. Undeterred, he fired three-quarters of a drum at the bomber before suffering a stoppage which he was unable to clear. As his second Lewis also refused to function, he had no choice but to return to base to have the trouble put right.

The R.25 was now in trouble. The Camels' fire had put one of its engines out of action and some of its instruments had also been smashed. Although unable to maintain height with a full bomb load, and with their speed down to about 60 mph, the crew decided to press on to London. The Giant's bombs fell in open ground near Wanstead. Up to this point the R.25 had been harried by Bob Hall, who was able to fire only five rounds before each stoppage; he now lost his target, but encountered the R.39 a few miles to the west.

The R.25 scraped home to Ostende, having survived successive attacks by five fighters. They had collectively fired over 800 rounds at her, and after landing she was found to have taken no fewer than 88 hits. Had the fighters not suffered continual gun stoppages, there seems little doubt that they would have brought down the bomber. However, there were other factors in their failure to do so; analysing the action later, the Camel pilots of No 44 Squadron realized that the Giant's sheer size had led them to believe that they had been firing from a much closer range than was actually the case. Instead of closing to within 50 yards, as they had thought at the time, they must have been anything up to 250 yards away.

Meanwhile, in Flanders – and, indeed, along the whole of the Western Front – the first month of 1918 had passed quietly.

32

The weather had not been conducive to offensive operations, and air activity had been mostly restricted to routine observation flights.

It was a situation that would not last for much longer.

CHAPTER THREE

Air operations during February 1918 were once again severely hampered by bad weather, but on the few favourable flying days there were some spirited combats between the opposing sides, the RFC's pilots often finding themselves outnumbered. Most of the activity took place in the second half of the month, and the following extracts from the operations record of No 43 Squadron – then based at La Gorgue under the command of Major C. C. Miles – are fairly representative of fighter operations during this period.

'*17 February*. Trollope's patrol of five Camels encountered an enemy formation of eight machines. As a result of the combat which ensued three enemy machines were driven down out of control.'

'*18 February*. Captain Trollope while on a special mission (alone) saw three Armstrong Whitworths under attack by six enemy machines. He at once attacked the enemy who were then joined by six more. Trollope fought the twelve for ten minutes until all his ammunition was exhausted, by which time the enemy machines had all flown away to the east.'

'*19 February*. Second Lieutenant R. J. Owen whilst on patrol on his own was attacked by five enemy scouts in the vicinity of the Bois de Biez. He fought the five, one of which according to the testimony of anti-aircraft gunners was seen to fall in flames.'

'*26 February*. Captain Trollope leading a patrol of nine Camels saw four DFWs escorted by fifteen enemy Scouts. He led the patrol into the attack. Although gun trouble prevented him from joining in he stayed in the middle of the fight and saw two enemy machines crash and a third fall out of control.'

In the Verdun sector, René Fonck of SPA 3 *Cigognes* had a curious encounter during the third week of February with a German two-seater nicknamed *Fantomas* by the French. The aircraft was an LVG with distinctive markings – the nature of which is unfortunately unrecorded – and during the winter of 1917–18 its unnamed crew had become notorious for their highly accurate trench strafing attacks. In November 1917 an SPA 3 pilot named René Montrion claimed to have shot the troublesome LVG down, but it cropped up again shortly afterwards and continued to put in frequent appearances, despite subsequent claims to its destruction. Then, one cold February morning, René Fonck caught the LVG as it was approaching the French lines, doubtless intent on yet another strafing run. This time there was no mistake, and the burning remains of *Fantomas* were scattered over no-man's land.

During the early weeks of 1918, the Air Staff in London had been giving considerable thought to the expansion of an RFC bombing force to undertake long-range attacks on German industrial targets and communications. Such a force already existed in embryo; in September 1917 the 41st Wing RFC, comprising three squadrons under the command of Lieutenant Colonel C. L. N. Newall, had been formed specifically to undertake attacks on German targets in response to the Gotha raids on the British mainland. Of the three units, No 55 Squadron was equipped with de Havilland DH4s for the day bombing role, while Nos 100 (FE2bs) and 16 RNAS (Handley Page 0/100s) Squadrons were reserved for night bombing.

The 41st Wing's first attack was carried out on 17 October 1917 by No 55 Squadron against the large steelworks at Saarbrücken-Burbach. Eleven DH4s took off from Ochey and eight of them attacked the target, killing four people, injuring nine and causing 17,500 marks worth of damage. On 21 October the same squadron sent out twelve DH4s to bomb factories and railyards at Bous, on the Moselle north of Hagendingen and about sixty miles from the squadron's base. One aircraft turned back with engine trouble, but the remainder pressed on and bombed the objective from 15,000 feet. On the way home from the target the DH4s were attacked by ten Albatros Scouts but managed to beat them off, claiming four enemy aircraft destroyed for the loss of one DH4. Only one of the latter was lost; its pilot, Captain Daniel Owen, succeeded in landing behind the German lines despite being severely wounded in the left eye.

This operation highlighted the excellent qualities of the DH4, a highly versatile aircraft which, to the RFC, was in many ways what Geoffrey de Havilland's Mosquito was to be to the Royal Air Force in the Second World War. Powered by a 160 hp Rolls-Royce III or V engine, it had a top speed of 117 mph, an endurance of three and a half hours and had a good defensive armament of one fixed forward-firing Vickers gun and either one or two Lewis guns in the rear cockpit. Its maximum bomb load was two 230-lb or four 112-lb bombs, or an equivalent weight of smaller weapons.

Designed from the outset for high-speed bombing, the DH4 was far more effective than the FE2b, which had originated as a fighter. The FE had fought well against the Fokker Mono-plane in the summer of 1916, but it had soon become outclassed by a new generation of German fighters such as the Albatros and had been introduced to the night bombing role. Its 120 hp Beardmore engine gave it a top speed of barely 80 mph. As it was a 'pusher' type, its observer sat in the extreme nose, operating a forward-firing Lewis gun and a second Lewis on a telescopic mounting over the wing centre section firing upwards and rearwards. It could carry one 230-lb or three 112-lb bombs. The cockpit layout provided excellent visibility when conditions were good, but in the winter the crew often had difficulty in locating their targets because they were blinded by rain or sleet. Sometimes, they arrived back at base so stiff and numb with cold that they had to be lifted from their positions. Despite its drawbacks, however, the FE2b was to continue in service with No 100 Squadron until August 1918.

The 41st Wing's third bomber type, the Handley Page 0/100 – which equipped No 16 (Naval) Squadron – owed its origins to a requirement, issued in December 1914, for a 'bloody paraly-ser of an aeroplane' for the bombing of Germany. The nick-name subsequently bestowed on it by its crews was inevitable, but the 'bloody paralyser' adequately met, and in some cases exceeded, its requirements in the role it was intended to perform. Powered by two Rolls-Royce Eagle II engines, it had a speed of around 75 mph and carried a four-man crew, with positions for single or twin Lewis machine-guns in nose and dorsal locations and another Lewis firing downward and rearward through a trap in the floor. It could carry sixteen 112-lb or eight 250-lb bombs internally, two and a half times the load it had been designed to lift. The 0/100 had entered service with No 3 Wing RNAS on the Western Front in November 1916, and from the spring of the following year its two squadrons, Nos 14 and 16, had concentrated on the night bombing of major German installations such as U-boat bases, railway stations and industrial centres. Consequently, when No 16 Squadron was detached to form part of the 41st Wing in September, it brought considerable experience with it.

The first operation of the 41st Wing's night bombers was flown on 24 October 1917, when, on a squally, blustery night, nine 0/100s and sixteen FE2bs took off from Ochey, the Handley Pages to attack the Burbach works and the FEs to bomb railyards between Falkenburg and Saarbrücken. No 16 Squadron failed to locate the target and two of the 0/100s failed to return, but No 100 Squadron's FEs reported several direct hits on their objective, including one on a train by a 230-lb bomb.

During its first month of operations the 41st Wing carried out eight raids and dropped over eleven tons of bombs, but with the onset of bad weather in November only five more raids could be undertaken before the end of the year. There was no doubt by this time that the enemy regarded the 41st Wing's efforts as more than just a nuisance, for they bombed Ochey twice in November and twice in December. During the night attack of 4/5 December, they damaged sixteen of the Wing's aircraft.

Sporadic raids on German targets resumed in January 1918, but because of the weather and various other factors these were mostly short-range affairs. On 1 February the status of the 41st Wing was upgraded and it was redesignated VIII Brigade, Newall being promoted to the rank of brigadier general. At the same time, work began on getting three new night bomber and three day bomber airfields ready for operations.

On 18/19 February No 100 Squadron flew its longest-range mission so far, sending eleven FEs out to attack Trier, a round trip of 200 miles. Some of the aircraft flew so low over the town that the German anti-aircraft gunners were compelled to cease firing for fear of their shells causing more damage to Trier than the raiders' bombs. The next day it was the turn of No 55 Squadron, which despatched ten DH4s under Captain J. B. Fox to Mannheim, with Kaiserslautern as an alternative target. The mission got away to a bad start when one of the DH4s got out of control in cloud at 5,000 feet and went into a spin; the pilot recovered at 1,000 feet and returned to base, severely shaken and in an overstressed aircraft. A second aircraft lost contact with the rest of the formation and it also returned. Over no-man's land, the other DH4s ran into a very strong and unexpected headwind that cut down their ground speed so much that it soon became obvious that they would not reach either of their selected targets. They therefore bombed Pirmasens, between Saarbrücken and Karlsruhe, which was the principal production centre of German army boots. All the attacking aircraft returned safely to Ochey, having encountered no opposition from either anti-aircraft fire or fighters.

Meanwhile, General Erich Ludendorff's staff were putting the finishing touches to the plan for their spring offensive. Ludendorff knew that his marginal superiority of 200 divisions against 175 would not be enough to sustain an offensive in more than one sector of the front. The whole plan depended on a single swift hammer-blow; the problem lay in selecting the spot on which the full weight of the blow was to fall. Some of Ludendorff's staff officers advocated striking against the French, but Ludendorff objected; he pointed out that if the French were defeated the British would almost certainly go on fighting, but if the British were defeated the French would probably give in. Besides, the French were more manoeuvrable than the British, experienced in fluid rather than static warfare; it might prove hard to effect a complete breakthrough in their sectors. There was no doubt in Ludendorff's mind that the blow must be directed against the British.

As February gave way to March, the German divisions that were to take part in the attack swung forward to their jumping-off positions. Seldom, since the early months of the war, had the morale of the German troops been so high. As the time of the attack approached, officers and men were fully briefed on what was expected of them, so that there was no room for rumour or doubt. So thoroughly had all the preparations been made that failure was regarded as an impossibility. If the attack should be held up at any one point, operations were to cease there immediately and the troops switched to another sector.

Four army groups were deployed between Arras and La Fère. The most northerly was known as the Mars Group; this was detailed to meet and parry any counter-attack from the direction of Arras, so protecting the flank of the first main attacking army. This was the 17th Army under General Otto von Below; code-named Michael I, it was to be launched against Croisilles and Bullecourt. By mid-March, the strength of the German Flying Corps operating in support of the 17th Army had virtually doubled to include seventeen reconnaissance *Staffeln*, seven *Schlachtstaffeln* (ground-attack squadrons), thirteen *Jagdstaffeln* and three bomber *Staffeln*. These units were deployed on thirty-one airfields in the Lille area.

Immediately south of Michael I was the 2nd Army under General von der Marwitz, code-named Michael II; this was directed against Bapaume and Péronne. In support of the 2nd Army were sixteen reconnaissance *Staffeln*, eleven *Schlachtstaffeln*, ten *Jagdstaffeln* and three bomber *Staffeln*, deployed on thirty-three airfields in the area to the east of Cambrai and St Quentin.

Finally, in the area around St Quentin itself, was the 18th Army (Michael III) under General Oskar von Hutier, its strength substantially bolstered by the speedy transfer of the reserve divisions of the Crown Prince of Prussia from the Champagne Front north-east of Châlons. The 18th Army was supported by sixteen reconnaissance *Staffeln*, nine *Schlachtstaffeln*, twelve *Jagdstaffeln* and six bomber *Staffeln*. Its task was to drive a wedge between the French and British armies; the latter would then be encircled and destroyed by the two northern German army groups.

The number of *Staffeln* engaged in support of a particular army would fluctuate somewhat as the offensive developed, and air units were switched from one sector to another as required. By the third week of March, the Germans had air superiority on the Somme, with 730 aircraft, including 326 fighters, opposing 579 Royal Flying Corps machines, of which 261 were fighters. Opposite the French sectors the Germans had a further 367 aircraft of all types; the French Aviation Militaire, as it was now known, had some 2,000 aircraft of all types in service at this time, but no accurate figure exists for the numbers deployed in any given sector.

The weight of the German offensive was to fall on the British 3rd and 5th Armies. On 20 March, the former had eight divisions in the line and seven in reserve; the latter had eleven divisions in the line, with three infantry and three cavalry divisions in reserve. In support of the 3rd Army was the RFC's III Brigade, comprising the 12th (Corps) Wing under Lieutenant Colonel Mitchell and the 13th (Army) Wing under Lieutenant Colonel Playfair. The 12th Wing comprised Nos 12, 13, 15 and 59 Squadrons, all with RE8s; the 13th Wing comprised No 3 Squadron (Camels), Nos 11 and 22 Squadrons (Bristol Fighter), No 41 Squadron (SE5a), Nos 43 and 46 Squadrons (Camel), No 49 Squadron (DH4), Nos 56, 60 and 64 Squadrons (SE5a), No 70 Squadron (Camel) and No 102 Squadron, which was a night flying unit equipped with FE2bs.

The 5th Army was supported by the RFC's V Brigade, consisting of the 15th (Corps) Wing under Lieutenant Colonel Charlton and the 22nd (Army) Wing under Lieutenant Colonel Holt. The 15th Wing comprised Nos 8, 35 and 82 Squadrons with F.K.8s, and Nos 52 and 53 Squadrons with RE8s, while the 22nd Wing comprised No 5 (Naval) Squadron with DH4s, No 23 Squadron with SPADs, Nos 24 and 84 Squadrons with SE5as, No 48 Squadron with Bristol Fighters, No 54 Squadron with Camels and No 101 Squadron with FE2bs for night flying.

The British had plenty of warning of the impending assault. As March wore on the German air effort intensified, although it was hampered by increasingly bad weather, and there were a number of brisk engagements between opposing fighters. On 12 March the Richthofen *Geschwader* engaged and destroyed four out of nine Bristol Fighters of No 62 Squadron, which was operating north of Arras as part of the 9th Wing. The next day, farther south in 13th Wing's sector, seven Camels of No 43 Squadron, escorting a pair of F.K.8s, encountered a mixed force of fifteen Albatros and Pfalz Scouts and immediately attacked them; Captain Henry Woollett fired at one, which broke up in mid-air, then engaged a second, which went out of control and crashed. Two more were shot down by 2nd

Lieutenant Peiler, and one each by 2nd Lieutenants Lingham, Lomax, King and Dean. A ninth enemy aircraft was shot down by the observer in one of the F.K.8s – which belonged to No 2 Squadron – and the remainder prudently decided to break off the engagement and head for home.

On 17 March, Captain John Trollope, also of No 43 Squadron, sighted six enemy scouts while flying alone on a 'height test'. He climbed above them and attacked, sending one down out of control. The other five dived away. Shortly afterwards, while returning to base, Trollope sighted four more enemy aircraft and attacked one of them at close range. It caught fire and broke up. Trollope at once turned to engage the rest, but they flew away eastwards at high speed.

The day before that, there had been a clear indication that the Germans were concentrating their best units to the south of Lille, which hitherto had been the Richthofen *Geschwader*'s normal operating area, when pilots of No 4 (Australian) Squadron encountered the brightly-painted Albatros Scouts near Douai. The Squadron, operating from Bruay as part of the 10th (Army) Wing, sent out seven Camels that morning to bomb objectives near Douai with their 20-lb bombs; they had just carried out their attack and were climbing back to 16,000 feet when they were attacked by Richthofen's pilots. Twelve Albatros attacked in twos and threes, four remaining above the Australians to watch for stragglers. The flight commander, Lieutenant G. F. Malley, and Lieutenant C. M. Feez avoided the first pass and went in pursuit of two red Albatros, which were diving in formation. The Australians shot both of them down. Meanwhile, Lieutenant A. W. Adams, some 2,000 feet lower down, fought a hectic battle with two more scouts and shot one down. Lieutenant W. H. Nicholls, chased down to ground level, was forced to land his Camel in the German lines and was taken prisoner, while Lieutenant P. K. Schafer, attacked by three Albatros, dropped 10,000 feet in a spin before recovering and making his escape. He landed at Bruay with sixty-two bullet holes in his Camel.

On 18 March, a German NCO pilot, forced down and captured, admitted under interrogation that the offensive would begin on 20 or 21 March. On the evening of the 20th, RFC observation aircraft, taking advantage of a break in the weather, returned with the intelligence that enemy troops in the front line were being relieved by fresh units, a sure sign that an attack was about to develop. The 3rd and 5th Armies were placed on alert, their front shrouded in thick mist.

At 4.45 am, the German artillery opened up with a furious barrage of high explosive and gas shells that blasted the full length of the British line. Long-range guns also bombarded supply dumps and lines of communication far to the rear, up to twenty-eight miles behind the front line. More than fifty miles of the British front, from Monchy to Tergnier, was flooded with poison gas. All known or suspected gun positions were attacked with the aim of weakening the defensive shell curtain and counter-battery fire, and all ground likely to be sheltering reserves was smothered. Then, out of the mist, in the wake of a high-explosive barrage, fifty-six German divisions hurled themselves forward into the attack.

General Gough's 5th Army, outnumbered four to one, was soon reduced to isolated units, making their last stands far behind the forward German echelons, their surviving artillery fighting close-range actions over open sights. For several vital hours neither the men in the forward positions, nor the staff officers at Brigade, Division, Corps and even Army Head-quarters had any real idea what was happening. Communica-tions had been severed by the preliminary artillery onslaught; frantic light signals went unobserved in the fog, which also rendered air reconnaissance impossible. On the left, General Byng, commanding the 3rd Army, was a little more fortunate; an RE8 of No 59 Squadron was able to monitor the course of the battle for more than an hour after first light before it was destroyed by a shell.

About mid-morning, the mist thinned sufficiently to allow more reconnaissance sorties to be flown. There followed a stream of signals from excited RFC crews, indicating a profu-sion of targets ranging from roads clogged with masses of German infantry to gun batteries being brought into action or moving forward. For the first time, air observation revealed the extent of the disaster that had befallen the two British armies. Every available RFC aircraft that could carry bombs was at once thrown into the attack, but operations were hampered throughout 21 March by the continual adverse weather, which was worst in 5th Army's area. All day long, the aircrews flew through shifting veils of fog and mist that would part briefly for a few seconds to reveal enemy forces pushing relentlessly across country from St Quentin. The squadrons co-operating with the 5th Army attacked wherever and whenever they were able, while the Corps squadrons did their best to provide the British artillery with worthwhile targets.

To make matters worse, many of the forward RFC airfields were now within range of enemy gunfire, and some were even in danger of being overrun. By nightfall on 22 March, seventeen squadrons had been compelled to evacuate their aerodromes and move back to safer locations, having first destroyed anything that might be of use to the enemy.

Confused and sporadic air operations continued throughout the 22nd. A patrol of No 2 (Australian) Squadron on this day was perhaps typical of many experiences along the battle area. Ten SE5as set out to patrol St Quentin; two had to turn back with engine trouble, but the other eight encountered five enemy two-seaters escorted by a number of single-seaters. Lieutenant Forrest dived on a two-seater, which burst into flames, and Lieutenant McKenzie sent an Albatros down out of control. Turning north along the front, the Australians passed over Bourlon Wood, where they spotted five German triplanes below. Captain Phillips attacked the leader, who rolled over and went into a slow spin; the other triplanes scattered in the haze. Over Bullecourt more Albatros Scouts were engaged; Lieutenant Forrest shot down two out of control and Lieutenant Holden got a third.

On 23 March, as the weather began to clear somewhat, order started to emerge from the overall confusion and, for the first time, the RFC found itself in a position to influence the course of the battle. A magnificent defence by the British infantry divisions in the centre of the 3rd Army's front, south-east of Arras, kept the line intact, but the right wing near Bapaume was hard-pressed and fighting a desperate rearguard action as the troops strove to maintain contact with the fragmented and retreating 5th Army. It was in this sector, on the 23rd, that some of the most intensive air operations took place.

The Camels of No 4 (Australian) Squadron were in the thick of the fighting here. That morning the Squadron was detailed to attack the enemy near Vaux-Vraucourt and along the Bapaume–Cambrai road. Two flights of six Camels took off just after 10.00 am, led by Captain Courtney, and flew to their targets at low level, under 500 feet all the way. Their arrival took the German troops by surprise, the bombing and strafing attack throwing the marching soldiers and their horse-drawn transport into confusion. Top cover during the initial attack was provided by Lieutenant G. F. Malley's six Camels, which were hotly engaged by several Albatros. Malley shot down two, and 2nd Lieutenant Scott a third. Later in the day, the same squadron raided Bapaume, which had been captured by the enemy. The Camels dropped their bombs on British ammunition dumps which had not been destroyed and then climbed to engage a formation of German fighters. The first Australian to meet them, Lieutenant A. E. Robertson, shot down one Fokker Triplane and drove two others down out of control.

The strafing attacks were already beginning to have an effect on the Germans, as the war diary of the 73rd Regiment, describing events of 22 March, reveals.

'The English got valuable support from their aircraft which attacked regardless of consequences. The squadrons, flying very low, found profitable targets for bomb and machine-gun in the thickly concentrated masses of the 111th Regiment . . . about a dozen English low-flying aircraft whizzed up and from an incredibly low height bombed our advancing troops. This caused great confusion . . .'

The following day, Sunday 24 March, was critical. Some fighter squadrons, which had been operating from bases a distance from the battle area, were now moved closer to it in order to provide escort for the all-important ground attack and observation aircraft, and to establish the air superiority that was so vital to the success of the RFC's effort. One of them was No 43 Squadron, which moved from La Gorgue, near Merville, to Avesnes-le-Comte near Arras.

On the first patrol of 24 March, Captain John Trollope, leading a flight of Camels, sighted three DFW two-seaters and worked his way round to the east to cut off their line of escape. He closed in and fired at the first, but then his guns jammed. After clearing the stoppage he engaged the second DFW and fired 100 rounds at it, seeing it break up in mid-air; he at once closed on the third and set it on fire. Meanwhile, the first DFW had been engaged by Captain Cecil King and 2nd Lieutenant A. P. Owen, who harried it between them until it broke up. Some Albatros Scouts turned up belatedly to protect the DFWs, and Trollope immediately shot one down. Lower down, another flight of 43 Squadron Camels led by Captain Henry Woollett was busy attacking more DFWs, one of which he set on fire. Lieutenant Daniel of Woollett's flight, losing contact with his leader during the engagement, joined up with No 3 (Naval) Squadron, which attacked five Pfalz Scouts. Daniel destroyed one of them, bringing No 43 Squadron's total for that patrol to seven.

That afternoon Trollope led a second patrol into action, despite deteriorating weather conditions. Soon after crossing the front line he sighted four enemy two-seaters attacking a pair of RE8s; five or six German single-seat fighters were also in the vicinity. Trollope led his pilots down to the aid of the REs and he singled out one of the two-seaters, firing in short bursts as he closed in to almost point-blank range. He saw pieces fly off the enemy's wing and then the whole wing collapsed. Turning hard, Trollope came round for a stern attack on a second two-seater, braving fierce defensive fire from a determined rear gunner as he did so. A few moments later the German observer was dead in his cockpit and his aircraft spiralling earthwards in flames. Almost immediately Trollope latched on to a third two-seater which was flying very close to the ground; a short burst from his guns and it nose-dived into the earth, disintegrating on impact.

'I then saw one of our fellows attacked by twelve Huns,' Trollope reported later, 'so I climbed up to him and let him get away but then I ran out of ammunition and turned for home but not before being able to confirm that two enemy scouts, attacked by 2nd Lieutenants Owen and Highton, respectively, had crashed.'

During the afternoon, No 43 Squadron's pilots fired 6,800 rounds in the course of strafing attacks on enemy troops by nine Camels led by Henry Woollett, who also shot down two enemy observation balloons in flames.

By the end of that Sunday, Lieutenant 'Bert' Hull, No 43

Squadron's records officer, could report to his CO, Major Miles, that the unit had broken all its previous records, having destroyed twenty-two enemy aircraft without loss in the day's fighting, and that the destruction of six by Captain Trollope in a single day had created a new RFC/RNAS record.

Four days later, it was Hull's sadder duty to report that Captain Trollope, together with 2nd Lieutenants Adams, Maasdorp, Prier and Owen, was missing, and that Cecil King had been wounded. King had come back to report that, after attacking two DFWs, he had climbed to assist John Trollope who was under attack by eight enemy scouts. Though King had shot one down, he had been unable to extricate his friend from the battle.

John Trollope, his left hand shattered, crash-landed in the enemy lines and was taken prisoner. In a German hospital his hand was amputated above the wrist. A sick man, he was repatriated towards the end of June, arriving home soon after the award of a Bar to his Military Cross had been announced in recognition of his exploit on 24 March. The six aircraft he had destroyed on that day brought his total to sixteen. He was twenty years old. Later, his arm had to be amputated at the shoulder, but despite his infirmity he built a successful career for himself in civilian life. During the Second World War, he applied to rejoin the Royal Air Force, was accepted and took up an administrative post with RAF Maintenance Command.

Again, the war diaries of the German units involved in the offensive bear witness to the growing effectiveness of the RFC's onslaught on 24 March. The diary of the 100th Grenadier Regiment states that 'Early in the day the First and Second 100th were ordered to assemble near Athies and suffered losses of eight officers and 125 men in a few seconds from air bombs', while an account in the war record of the 8th Grenadier Regiment is even more descriptive.

'As we were moving forward after crossing the Somme, there suddenly appeared before us some twenty British aeroplanes which dived to a height of about 100 metres and then, continuing to two to three metres off the ground, attacked us with their machine-guns. Several Tommies flew so low that their wheels touched the ground. My company commander, Lieutenant Nocke, had to fling himself flat, but for all that he was struck on the back by the wheels of one machine, thus being literally run over. Not far from me an aeroplane appeared at about one metre from the ground making straight for me and for the moment I did not know in what direction to throw myself; the pilot appeared determined to run over me.'

The next day, 25 March, was also a time of crisis. At 7.30 am, the crew of a No 59 Squadron RE8 reported very large concentrations of enemy infantry just east of Bapaume and requested heavy artillery fire, but the call remained unanswered. By this time, part of the area covered by the right of the British 5th Army had been taken over by units of the French 3rd Army, hastily thrown into the battle, but they too came under very heavy pressure and were relentlessly driven back. By the afternoon, the whole Allied line was crumbling.

It was time for desperate measures. With the Germans sweeping on in the north through Ervillers, in the centre to the outskirts of Thiepval and Montauban down to the Somme at Ham, and in the south towards Hattencourt, Champien and Noyon, Amiens itself – the main British supply and communications base – must surely fall if the enemy drive were not checked quickly. Early that afternoon, after consulting with the Chief of the Air Staff, Sir Hugh Trenchard, the C-in-C of the RFC in France, Major General Salmond, issued a dramatic directive to the commander of the IX (GHQ) Brigade, which had not yet been fully committed to the battle but held as a reserve force.

'I wish you,' Salmond said, 'as soon as you can after receipt of this, to send out your Scout squadrons on to the line Grevilliers–Martinpuich–Maricourt. These squadrons will bomb and shoot up everything they can see on the enemy's side of the line. Very low flying is essential. All risks to be taken. Urgent.'

The Brigade's 9th Wing, comprising Nos 25 and 27 Squadrons (DH4), No 62 Squadron (Bristol Fighter), Nos 73 and 80 Squadrons (Camel) and No 79 Squadron (Dolphin) responded magnificently, flying as long as the light lasted, bombing and strafing the enemy columns, flying back to base to reload and then returning to repeat the process. Hitherto, most of the bombing and strafing had been directed against the Germans'

47

infantry reserves, and this new assault on their communication routes left them severely shaken. 'Hostile airmen, flying low, delay the march with machine-gun fire and bombs,' wrote the diarist of the 52nd Reserve Regiment. 'Hostile airmen are present in crowds. We count more than 30 above us at the same time . . . Airmen came down to 20 metres in order to release their bombs. One Grenadier regiment has suffered such casualties that it has had to be relieved.'

The battle was also joined by squadrons of I Brigade's 10th (Army) Wing, which at this time included two Sopwith Camel squadrons: Major McLaughry's No 4 Squadron, Australian Flying Corps, and No 3 Squadron Royal Naval Air Service, which was commanded by Major Raymond Collishaw. 'Collie', as he was nicknamed, was a Canadian from Nanaimo, British Columbia. A born adventurer – he had been a member of the support team which had accompanied Captain Scott's ill-fated Antarctic Expedition in 1912 – he had been twenty-one years old at the outbreak of the First World War, and had immediately given up his career as a seaman to volunteer for pilot duties with the RNAS.

Collishaw first went to France flying a Sopwith Pup on escort missions. Changing to Sopwith 1½-Strutters, he scored his first victory on 12 October 1916, shooting down a Fokker Monoplane near Oberndorf. Two weeks later he destroyed two more enemy aircraft in a single sortie, an exploit that earned him the French *Croix de Guerre*. Because of the promise he showed as a pilot and fighter leader, he was allowed to form a Canadian Flight of No 10 RNAS Squadron. He had always been impressed by the distinctive markings adopted by many German fighter pilots, so he had the Flight's Sopwith Triplanes doped black all over and bestowed names on them: 'Black Death', 'Black Roger', 'Black Sheep' and 'Black Prince'. His own triplane was named 'Black Maria'.

The 'Black Flight' quickly became renowned along the front, its five pilots notching up respectable scores, often in combat with the Richthofen *Geschwader*. In June 1917 one of them, Lieutenant J. E. Nash from Hamilton, Ontario, was shot down and killed by Karl Allmenroeder, the German ace, who in turn was shot down and killed by Collishaw on the 25th of that month. By the time Collishaw was sent home to Canada for a rest in July, his personal score stood at thirty-seven enemy aircraft destroyed.

Returning to the Western Front in November, Collishaw was appointed CO of No 13 Squadron RNAS, one of the units responsible for the air defence of Dunkirk, and shot down three more enemy aircraft on 1 December. He assumed command of No 3 Squadron RNAS shortly after Christmas, but since squadron commanders were forbidden to fly on operations for a time he had no further opportunity to add to his score, and it was June 1918 before he was able to resume operational flying.

At the time of the Ludendorff Offensive the 10th Wing also had one SE5a squadron, No 40. This, too, was led by a distinguished pilot and commander, Major Roderic Dallas, an Australian. Dallas had also started his war as an RNAS pilot in 1915, flying Nieuport Scouts with No 1 Squadron, and had become something of a celebrity the following May by shooting down a pair of twin-engined Friedrichshafen bombers in the Dunkirk sector. At the end of the year No 1 Squadron had exchanged its Nieuports for Sopwith Triplanes, and in 1917 – now under Dallas's leadership – had fought with considerable success against the elite German *Jagdgeschwader*, including Richthofen's. By the end of the year, when he was rested, Dallas had scored twenty-six confirmed victories. Returning to the Western Front after a spell on home defence duties, he was given command of No 40 Squadron, which at once found itself in the thick of the fighting.

The usual tactics involved cratering the roads with bombs, after which the pilots would strafe the German traffic as it tried to circumvent the holes. The pilots were aided in their task by the fact that the ground on either side of the approach roads was wet and boggy, causing fearful congestion. The troops could and did scatter, but regimental horse transport drawing stores, field kitchens, heavy machine-guns, mortars and reserves of ammunition had to stand under fire. Young pilots, from the English shires and the Dominions alike, openly admitted to weeping in their cockpits on the flight home from the battle area, their minds harrowed by the vision of the carnage their bombs and bullets had wrought among the luckless animals.

Losses from ground fire were heavy, and most aircraft

returned to base with holes in them. The German Flying Corps attempted to disrupt the attacks on numerous occasions, but were usually heavily engaged and beaten off by the Allied fighters. On 25 March, for example, a flight of six Camels of No 4 (Australian) Squadron was attacked by a mixed formation of enemy aircraft as it was completing a strafing attack; two Fokker Triplanes and an Albatros were promptly shot down by Lieutenant A. E. Robertson, while another pilot destroyed a two-seater. The Australian squadron lost two pilots that day, one of whom was taken prisoner, and three more were wounded, all the casualties being caused by ground fire.

At night, the offensive against the enemy supply lines was continued by the FE2bs of Nos 101, 102 and 83 Squadrons, the latter having arrived at St Omer from England on 6 March and moved up to Auchel the next day. The crews flew through storms of hail and snow to bomb road and rail junctions at Péronne, Bapaume and half a dozen other places.

By 26 March the pressure on the 3rd Army lifted, thanks to the continued air attacks and to extremely stubborn resistance by the British troops, and in this sector the crisis was over; but the 5th Army, with orders to hold the approaches to Amiens, was in desperate straits. Its only reserves were 2,200 men from all manner of units, many of them non-combatant, commanded by an artillery officer who had been on his way back from leave when the German attack developed. The RFC squadrons supporting the battered remnants of the 5th Army fought magnificently from dawn to dusk in the ground-attack role, and after dark the bombing campaign was intensified. That night, two flights of No 58 Squadron (FE2bs) made twenty-five sorties and flew a total of fifty hours, a record that stood until the end of the war, while Nos 101 and 102 Squadrons were continually in action against Ham and Cambrai. Over 500 25-lb bombs were dropped on these targets in a seven-hour period, direct hits being obtained on a train, a canal bridge and transport columns.

The following day, 27 March, witnessed one of the bravest exploits to emerge from the air war over the Western Front. That morning, 2nd Lieutenant Alan McLeod, a Canadian pilot flying Armstrong Whitworth F.K.8s with No 2 Squadron RFC took off to bomb enemy transport south of Arras, with 2nd

Lieutenant A. W. Hammond as his observer. As they were beginning their attack, they were bounced by eight enemy scouts, almost certainly from Richthofen's *Jagdgeschwader* 1. In the ensuing battle McLeod positioned the F.K.8 with great skill, enabling Hammond to shoot down three of the enemy fighters as they made successive attacks. However, the Big Ack was heavily damaged in the fight and both officers repeatedly wounded. The floor of the rear cockpit was shot through and collapsed, the same burst of fire hitting the petrol tank and setting it ablaze. Despite his wounds – he had been hit five times by now – McLeod managed to climb out of his burning cockpit to stand precariously on the lower wing. Clinging to the edge of the cockpit with one hand, he kept hold of the control column with the other, although flames were licking fiercely around it, and side-slipped the aircraft so that the slipstream took the fire away from himself and Hammond, who was still firing from what was left of the rear cockpit.

McLeod succeeded in bringing the Armstrong Whitworth down to a heavy landing in no-man's land. By now Hammond had been hit six times and was helpless, and despite his own severe wounds and the fact that the wreck of the aircraft was coming under machine-gun fire from German troops, McLeod dragged him clear and into cover just as the aircraft's bombs began to explode amid the flames. McLeod then collapsed from loss of blood. Luckily, the plight of the two officers had been seen by some British soldiers, who braved the enemy fire to bring both of them to safety. McLeod was later awarded the Victoria Cross while lying gravely ill in hospital.

Hammond recovered from his wounds and received a Bar to his Military Cross. Sadly, McLeod was less fortunate; a few months later, still weak and ill, he succumbed to the influenza epidemic that swept across Europe at the war's end.

That night, flying in stormy weather, RFC and RNAS aircraft following up the day's air attacks by dropping 840 bombs on the enemy and firing 18,000 rounds of ammunition. But the German drive continued, and on 28 March a major assault was made on Arras. The approaching enemy columns were seen by RFC observation aircraft, however, and the attack was broken up by further bombing and strafing and some highly effective artillery support. Farther south the exhausted 5th Army was still under heavy pressure, but observation aircraft reported particularly dense columns of enemy infantry and, in the words of the war diary of No 52 Squadron – flying RE8s from Abbeville – 'our machines had a field day attacking columns in fours. Heavy casualties were inflicted on several enemy battalions.'

Although the battle was far from over, it was now clear that the German attack was beginning to lose its impetus. On the southern flank of the bulge created by the enemy advance, fresh divisions of the French Army were coming into the line to stand shoulder to shoulder with the original British forces between Noyon and Roye, and with them, from the Champagne sector, came vital support in the shape of the Aviation Militaire. Among the units allocated to the fighting in Picardy were the *Cigognes* – the name now encompassed both *Escadrilles* of GC 12, SPA 3 and SPA 103 – and GC 19, the latter now under the command of Captain Albert Deullin.

'All day long,' wrote René Fonck afterwards, 'the air was filled with the roar of engines. We flew so low that we almost touched the enemy's bayonets, watching the compact masses of troops wilt away before our machine-gun fire. The chaos was terrible. Panic-stricken horses charged in all directions, trampling soldiers underfoot.'

On 29 March, René Fonck, flying from Raray, the *Cigognes'* base near the river Oise, destroyed two more enemy aircraft. This brought his score to thirty-two, placing him one ahead of his rival, Charles Nungesser. Fonck appeared to have taken little pleasure in his new status as ace of aces; the slaughter in Picardy had brought about a profound change in him, and in his fellow pilots. Hitherto, war had been an impersonal affair for the most part; a burst of gunfire, a flash of flame streaking back from an enemy aircraft, a ribbon of smoke that marked its end. Somehow, the man in the cockpit had always seemed unreal. Now, for the first time, they were able to see the deadly effect of their bullets on human and animal flesh from a range of only yards, and they were sickened by it. The war, after March 1918, became something to be ended as quickly as possible.

CHAPTER FOUR

'The weather was fine and the visibility good. A total of 23 tons of bombs were dropped by night and 17 tons by day. Enemy aircraft were active south of the Somme, and enemy two-seaters were employed in low flying and firing at our troops. Several large formations of E.A. Scouts were also encountered at a height. Two hostile balloons were shot down, and one hostile machine was brought down in our lines by infantry, in addition to those accounted for by aerial combat.'

So ran the terse words of RAF Communiqué No 1, dated 1 April 1918. There was no sense of the dramatic in it; neither was there anything to indicate that the RFC and the RNAS had now ceased to exist, and by their amalgamation had given birth to a new Service.

For the thousands of officers and men who now found themselves members of the RAF, the overnight change of identity meant nothing at all. They were too busy fighting to take any notice of it.

The fighting on that first day of April was characterized by determined attempts by both sides to shoot down each other's ground attack and observation aircraft. One of the fiercest air battles, and the most one-sided, took place when a DH4 of No 57 Squadron, flown by Captain F. McD. Turner with 2nd Lieutenant A. Leach as his observer, was attacked by five Fokker Triplanes while on a photography sortie. Leach fired thirty rounds into one of them from a range of 100 yards and the triplane went down in flames. The remaining four were then joined by ten more triplanes and Albatros Scouts; Leach fired a complete drum into one of the latter, which was seen to turn over and break up in mid-air. The rest of the attackers sheered off and the DH4 made its escape into friendly territory.

Among the battles that raged up above, Captain G. E. H. McElroy, an Irish flight commander with No 24 Squadron, attacked three enemy scouts in his SE5a, closing to well within 100 yards of one before firing a burst of 100 rounds from both guns into it. It went into a slow spin and crashed north of Ignaucourt. Three days later the same pilot unhesitatingly attacked seven enemy fighters which he spotted flying eastwards over the lines and shot one of them down from fifty yards' range. Then, on 7 April, McElroy attacked one of three two-seaters, braving fierce defensive fire to shoot it up from fifty yards; it nose-dived into the ground. Shortly afterwards, flying through broken cloud at 3,000 feet, he sighted three SEs being attacked by five triplanes and fired twenty rounds into one of the Fokkers from point-blank range. It, too, went down and crashed.

Several other pilots who were to emerge among the top thirty British and Empire aces of the First World War added to their scores during the bitter fighting of early April over the Somme. Captain R. A. Little of No 203 Squadron – an Australian – fired 200 rounds into a Fokker Triplane on 1 April and saw its lower wing break off as it dived earthwards; on 6 April he attacked a two-seater from 200 yards and closed in to 20 yards, firing all the time until it disappeared into cloud. As it emerged he attacked it again, still from close range, and saw it fall in flames. The next day, Little's patrol of Camels was attacked by ten Fokker Triplanes, one of which he shot down out of control.

Two other top pilots, Henry Woollett of No 43 Squadron and Lieutenant D. R. MacLaren of No 46, specialized in attacks on enemy balloons, which had been directing accurate artillery fire on to British troops. Woollett fired sixty rounds into a balloon on 2 April and it went down in flames, the two observers jumping clear by parachute; he then attacked a second balloon which also fell in flames, but this time no one got out. By now the Germans were making frantic efforts to haul down a third balloon, but this too burst into flames after Woollett had fired about fifty rounds into it. Balloon attacks of this kind were not popular, as the sites were always heavily defended, and sometimes the balloons were not easy to shoot down. On 3 April, for example, MacLaren and another 46 Squadron pilot, 2nd Lieutenant J. H. Smith, fired 300 rounds into one before its envelope finally collapsed and it dropped to earth.

During this period Richthofen's *Jagdgeschwader* was much in evidence over the deep salient created by the German advance, and on 6 April they gave No 43 Squadron a severe mauling. In the early afternoon the squadron was attacked by triplanes as it was ground strafing at Abancourt and destroyed four of them for the loss of one of its Camels, but on the next patrol three out of six Camels failed to return, and later in the day a fifth Camel was destroyed in a crash landing on the British side of the lines. The pilot of this aircraft (Lieutenant C. C. Banks), having shot down an Albatros, had returned to the main task of ground strafing when his Camel was badly hit by small-arms fire; despite having a holed petrol tank and no elevator control, he kept the battered machine in the air for two miles, just long enough to reach safety.

The second week of April began with pouring rain, and flying activity on both sides of the front was almost nil. On 9 April air operations were once again hampered by thick mist and drizzle, but despite the conditions the squadrons of I Brigade RAF reconnoitred the front and launched attacks wherever possible on German forces attacking between Bois Grenier and the La Bassée Canal. Nos 203 and 210 Squadrons – the old 'Naval 3' and 'Naval 10' Squadrons, given new identities on the formation of the RAF to avoid confusion with former RFC units bearing the same numbers – were much in evidence over the battlefield, providing cover for the ground-attack aircraft. Captain Little of No 203 Squadron shared in the destruction of a two-seater with two other pilots, while No 210 Squadron's Camels accounted for three more two-seaters and No 40 Squadron got one. All told, it had not been a good day for the *Schlachtflieger*, the German ground-attack crews.

Attacks on German ground forces continued throughout 10 April, again despite bad weather. Most of the German air activity also involved ground strafing, and there were few air combats, although Lieutenants H. L. Taylor and W. I. E. Lane of No 52 Squadron had a stiff fight when their RE8 was attacked by nine Fokker Triplanes. Lane, the observer, shot down one out of control, and although wounded he continued to engage the remainder and sent one of them down in flames. By this time the RE8 had suffered serious damage, but Taylor managed to crash-land it on the right side of the lines.

The next day began with low clouds and mist, which persisted until the middle of the afternoon. As soon as the cloud began to lift there was a sharp increase in air activity all along the front, particularly south of La Bassée. The SE5as of Major Roderic Dallas's No 40 Squadron were in the thick of the fighting in this sector, Dallas himself accounting for an enemy two-seater which he attacked with both guns down to a range of thirty yards. A few days later Dallas came very close to losing his life when his aircraft was badly hit by machine-gun fire from the ground. Although wounded in both legs he managed to reach base safely, and was back in action a fortnight later.

Two other pilots of No 40 Squadron also scored on 11 April. Late in the afternoon Captain G. H. Lewis, a flight commander, sighted seven Fokker Triplanes and attacked one of them, but was forced to break off when his guns jammed. Later, however, he encountered a solitary triplane and dived on it, firing long bursts with both guns until it went into a slow spin and crashed near Lens. The other pilot, Captain J. H. Tudhope, also attacked the formation of seven Fokkers, opening fire on one from very close range. His shooting was accurate and he saw several good bursts go home. The German pilot was probably hit, for the triplane jerked up into a stall and then spun into the ground.

The former Naval squadrons had a good day, too. Captain Little, leading No 203 Squadron into action against the German *Schlachtflieger* who were harassing Allied ground forces, attacked three two-seaters in company with the other Camels of his flight, and was in turn attacked by six Albatros Scouts which were providing top cover. Little turned to face them and shot one down, seeing it crash near Neuve Eglise. Meanwhile, Lieutenants A. T. Whealy and J. A. Glen had gone down to press home attacks on the two-seaters while the other Camels engaged their escorts; Whealy shot one down near Sailly-sur-Lys and another crashed in flames after Glen had fired 300 rounds into it.

In all the Germans lost eleven two-seaters during the day's fighting. The RAF suffered heavily too, the German fighters pressing home determined attacks on observation aircraft. Again, the courage of the RAF two-seater crews was typified by one battle in which Lieutenants R. G. Hart and L. F. Handford of No 15 Squadron, flying a contact patrol in their RE8, were savagely attacked by four Pfalz Scouts. Almost at once the RE's elevator and aileron controls were shot away. As the machine wallowed along, virtually helpless, Handford fired twenty rounds into the nearest Pfalz; both sets of wings broke off it and it burst into flames, crashing near Millencourt. Despite being wounded in the knee Handford engaged a second Pfalz, firing until he lost consciousness. British troops saw the enemy aircraft fall in flames behind the enemy lines. Another Pfalz followed the RE down to 100 feet, but broke off as the RAF aircraft crossed the front line. Hart managed to crash-land the crippled aircraft, using only rudder and throttle.

The next day, 12 April, was fine and clear throughout, with exceptional visibility, and the opposing sides engaged one another in a long series of fierce air battles. The RAF claimed forty-nine enemy aircraft during the day's fighting, and thirteen of them were destroyed by No 43 Squadron – six being accounted for by Captain Henry Woollett, who equalled John Trollope's earlier achievement. Woollett's terse combat report tells its own story.

'10.30 am. I led my patrol down on to eight EA just south-east of La Gorgue. I fired about 30 rounds into one single-seater; machine spun down and crashed just west of La Gorgue. I then dived on to another EA (a two-seater); this I saw crash just north-east of La Gorgue.

'I climbed up and got on the tail of an Albatros and after firing about 40 rounds it burst into flames, falling to pieces. I also saw another EA in flames, and also one crash which was shot down by Lt Daniel.

'5.00 pm. I led patrol down on to thirteen EA just north of La Gorgue. I fired about 30 rounds into one EA which was going east. This turned over on its back and fell to bits. I then climbed and got on to the tail of another Albatros; after firing several bursts into him, he spun down and crashed north-east of La Gorgue. On returning over lines I climbed up and found another EA at about 2,000 feet; this after about 20 rounds collapsed in the air and fell to bits. I saw two other EA crash, engaged by machines of my patrol.'

Throughout the day, aircraft of the RAF's I and II Brigades made low-level attacks on enemy forces between Wytschaete and the La Bassée Canal, while IX Brigade's fighters flew offensive patrols at altitude. Among the units engaged was No 74 Squadron, commanded now by the redoubtable Major Edward 'Mick' Mannock. Irish-born Mannock was not a gentleman in the accepted sense of the word. His boyhood had been marred by a constant struggle for survival. His father had been a corporal in the British Army, and in the late nineteenth century a corporal's pay did not stretch very far. To help his mother feed himself, his elder brother and elder sister, Mannock had been forced to leave school early and take a succession of jobs. At the age of twenty he had decided to see the world, working his way through the Middle East and Turkey, and on the outbreak of war he had immediately enlisted in the Army, joining the Medical Corps in the first instance. Chafing under a non-combatant role, he had applied to join the RFC, bluffing his way through medical examinations by memorizing eye-charts, for he had very poor vision in his left eye. He was accepted for flying training in 1916, and was fortunate to have as his instructor Captain James McCudden, a man who was already experienced in combat, and who did not care much about a man's background or political outlook as long as he had the makings of a good pilot. He taught Mannock all the tricks of his new trade, and the two became firm friends. It was a partnership that only death would sever.

Mannock joined No 40 Squadron in France early in 1917, and worked hard to improve his flying and shooting. Despite the handicap of his bad eye, he became a better than average marksman. Unlike many of his colleagues, he approached the science of air fighting with caution, preferring to skirt the fringes of his early air skirmishes rather than throw caution to the winds and dive into the middle of a fight. Some of his fellow pilots even began to hint that he lacked courage, but Mannock took no notice. He watched his more hot-headed critics go down in flames one after the other, and knew that he was right.

As soon as he was sure of his capabilities, he destroyed six enemy aircraft in three weeks, earning the Military Cross and rapid promotion to flight commander. Now that he had the attention of the other pilots, he set about forging a first-rate

58

fighting team, cultivating the complete trust of his men, never losing his head in action, always ensuring that the odds were in their favour before committing them to battle. He became a master of ambush, and before attacking an enemy he made certain that his pilots conformed to one golden rule of air fighting: always start the attack from above, seldom on the same level, and *never* from below. He taught his men to attack from astern, if possible, hitting the enemy on the first pass. He also taught them the full range of aerobatics to build up their confidence in handling their aircraft, at the same time stressing that aerobatics in a dogfight were useless and dangerous. Tight turns, he said, were the only manoeuvres that paid real dividends in an air battle.

His attitude towards the Germans was simple: he hated them with a deep, implacable loathing that intensified as the months went by. Once, when he was visiting No 56 Squadron's mess a few weeks after young Rhys-Davids shot down Werner Voss, someone got to his feet to make an impromptu speech in the middle of a party. He praised the qualities of the German pilots, then asked his colleagues to raise their glasses to the greatest enemy of all: Manfred von Richthofen. They all rose except Mannock, who pushed his glass aside with the words 'I won't drink to that bastard.'

Killing Germans was Mannock's sole obsession. When one of his own pilots failed to return a mood of icy rage would come over him and he would take to the air in search of vengeance. The sight of a German aircraft burning up as it fell seemed to hold a morbid fascination, not to say exultation, for him. 'Sizzle, sizzle – I sent one of the bastards to hell in flames today,' was his cry. Yet he had a horror of dying by fire. Before each flight he would carefully check his revolver to make sure it was loaded and in good working order. If he caught fire in the air, Mannock's way out was a bullet in the head.

By the beginning of 1918, when he was commanding No 74 Squadron, Mannock had destroyed fifty-six enemy aircraft, surpassing the score of his closest rival, James McCudden. 'Old Mac', as he was known to his pilots, levelled the score in February with the destruction of a Hanoveraner two-seater, but then he was sent back to England, where he was awarded the Victoria Cross. He was never to have an opportunity to gain further victories. After four months in England, McCudden was promoted and ordered back to France to take command of No 60 Squadron. On 9 July 1918 he crossed the Channel in his SE5a and landed at a French aerodrome to refuel before continuing to No 60's base. On take-off, his engine failed and McCudden disobeyed one of the cardinal laws of flying, a rule he had instilled over and over again into his students: if your engine fails on take-off, never turn back towards the airfield. He did so. His aircraft lost flying speed in the turn, stalled and went into a spin. Its pilot was killed instantly.

With Mannock in command, No 74 Squadron arrived in France on 30 March 1918 and installed itself a few days later at La Lovie, near Poperinghe, which it shared with the Camels of No 54 Squadron under Major R. S. Maxwell. Its first patrols were flown on 12 April, and on that day Mannock celebrated his return to action by shooting down two enemy aircraft.

The next few days were again obscured by low cloud and mist, followed by strong winds with snow and hail storms, so that very little flying was possible. In eight days the RFC squadrons claimed only eleven enemy aircraft and lost about an equal number of their own. Then, on 21 April, the weather cleared and the level of air activity rose correspondingly. Captain R. A. Little of No 203 Squadron was in action again, attacking the rear machine of a formation of twelve scouts which he encountered near Vieux Berquin; he watched it fall through 1,000 feet, apparently out of control, but was then himself attacked by six more scouts, which chased him through the formation he had just engaged. Little put the Camel into a spin, and just as he did so a burst of fire shot his controls away, leaving the machine completely unmanageable. Little sat there helpless, resigned to a violent death on impact, but then the spin flattened out with a jerk of such severity that it broke the fuselage under the pilot's seat. Little undid his seat belt and was hurled clear when the Camel struck the ground. Stunned but otherwise without serious hurt, he came to his senses to find that the enemy aircraft were taking it in turns to dive down and strafe him. Enraged, he drew his revolver and exchanged shots with one Albatros that came down to thirty feet.

After a few nerve-racking minutes the enemy aircraft were

driven off by rifle and machine-gun fire from the British positions close to where Little had crashed and where, shortly afterwards, he was gratefully sipping a mug of rum.

The Bristol Fighters of No 62 Squadron, which formed part of the 9th Wing, took part in the day's action. Second Lieutenant L. M. Thompson, the gunner in an aircraft flown by Lieutenant D. A. Savage, opened the score by shooting down an Albatros near Lille; soon afterwards the Bristol was attacked by two Pfalz and Thompson opened fire on one of them. It went into a vertical dive and broke up in the air, at which the third German flew off. Captain T. L. Purdon and 2nd Lieutenant P. V. G. Chambers, part of the same patrol, fired 100 rounds between them into a Fokker Triplane and saw it go into a steep spiral. It was finished off by 2nd Lieutenant W. E. Staton, also of No 62 Squadron, who saw it crash near Estaires.

But one combat overshadowed all others on that day, and enshrined 21 April 1918 in the annals of aviation history.

Shortly after ten o'clock that morning, Baron Manfred von Richthofen walked across the grass of Cappy aerodrome, the base of his *Jagdgeschwader* 1, towards his scarlet-painted Fokker Triplane. He had scored his eightieth victory the day before, and it seemed only a question of time before he would reach the magic total of one hundred.

By Richthofen's side trotted his black labrador, Moritz. Suddenly, an airman pointed a camera at the pair, intent on securing a snapshot to be treasured in years to come. Most German pilots considered it unlucky to be photographed just before a flight, but Richthofen laughed at such superstitions. He smiled as he turned to face the camera. The shutter clicked, and the Red Baron was photographed – for the last time.

As he was about to climb into his aircraft, another airman came up to him with a postcard he wanted to send home to his son. He asked the pilot to sign it. 'What's the matter?' asked Richthofen, smiling. 'Don't you think I'll come back?' He signed his name – for the last time.

Twenty miles away, at Bertangles aerodrome on the other side of the lines, the Sopwith Camels of No 209 Squadron RAF were running up their engines in readiness for take-off. In the cockpit of one of the fighters sat 24-year-old, Canadian-born Captain Roy Brown. A veteran pilot with the Distinguished

Service Cross and twelve kills to his credit, Brown presented a very different picture from Richthofen. Combat fatigue had taken its toll and had turned him into an old man. His face was sallow, and a nerve twitched at the corner of his mouth. He lived on brandy and milk, his tormented stomach constantly rejecting solid food. He gripped the joystick hard, desperately trying to stop his hand trembling. He felt sick and miserable. Yet this young, nerve-shattered man, within half an hour, would meet Germany's ace of aces in combat two miles above the earth in a duel that would leave only one survivor.

At 10.45, Richthofen led fifteen Fokker Triplanes westwards over the valley of the Somme. It was not long before they sighted a likely prey: two RE8 reconnaissance aircraft of No 3 Squadron, Australian Flying Corps, engaged in counter-battery work. Four triplanes broke away and dived down to attack them through a barrage of fire put up by British anti-aircraft guns. A couple of miles away, Captain Roy Brown saw the puffs of the shell-bursts and turned to investigate; a few moments later he picked out the two REs, being severely harassed by the triplanes, and led his eight Camels at full throttle to their rescue. Overhead, the remaining triplanes waited for an opportune moment to dive down and join the fray as soon as the Camels had committed themselves to engaging their four colleagues.

One of the Camel pilots was going into action for the first time. An old school friend of Brown's, his name was Lieutenant Wilfred R. May, better known to his fellow pilots as 'Wop'. Brown had told him not to get mixed up in a general dogfight, if one happened to develop, but to stay on the fringes and get in a shot if the chance presented itself. Now, as he watched the other Camels start their attack, May singled out a Fokker that looked like a sitting target and dived after it. He closed on it and opened fire, missing his target by a hopeless margin in his excitement and inexperience. As he tried to correct his aim his guns suddenly jammed; in his enthusiasm he had kept the triggers depressed for too long and the weapons had over-heated. Cursing himself, he broke off the chase and dived away towards the sanctuary of the British lines, again obeying Brown's earlier instructions.

From his vantage point above the mêlée, Richthofen had

seen the lone Camel break away. It was just the moment he had been waiting for, the kind of situation that had brought him so many victims. Putting his triplane into a shallow dive, he positioned himself on May's tail and gradually overhauled the British aircraft. Up above, Lieutenant Hans Wolff, whose task it was to guard Richthofen's tail at all times, was alarmed on seeing his leader dive towards the British lines and prepared to go after him. Just then, however, he was attacked by a Camel and compelled to take evasive action. When he shook off his adversary and looked down again, there was no sign of the scarlet triplane.

The first hint May had of any danger on his tail was the rattle of Richthofen's machine-guns. Later, he confessed to a feeling of sick horror as he twisted in his seat and saw the scarlet triplane only yards behind, the black-helmeted head of its pilot clearly visible behind the gunsight. He flung the Camel into a steep turn but failed to shake off his pursuer; Richthofen was too wily a hand to be thrown by basic manoeuvres of that sort.

High above, Roy Brown, who had been involved in a merry-go-round with half a dozen enemy fighters, suddenly found himself alone. Glancing down, he saw May's Camel and the scarlet triplane twisting and weaving along the Somme valley. Without hesitation, he dived down to the aid of his friend. By this time, May was virtually exhausted. He had tried everything to shake off his pursuer, and every move had failed. Richthofen continued to fire in economical short bursts, his bullets ripping through the fabric of the Camel's wings and sending up flurries of spray from the river. The speeding aircraft were down to less than 200 feet now as they flew along the course of the Somme.

'Just near Corbie,' May said later, 'von Richthofen beat me to it and came over the hill. At that point I was a sitting duck; I was too low down between the banks to make a turn away from him. I felt that he had me cold, and I was in such a state of mind at this time that I had to restrain myself from pushing the stick forward and diving into the river, as I knew that I had had it.'

Brown arrived just in time, pulling out of his dive above and slightly to the right of the Fokker. Correcting with rudder, he got the triplane squarely in his sights and opened fire with his twin Vickers. Bullets sewed a trail of holes along the triplane's fuselage. Richthofen looked around, and Brown clearly saw what he took to be an expression of startled fear on the face beneath the goggles. A moment later, the German pilot slumped sideways in the cockpit. The Fokker swerved violently, then righted itself and nosed over into a glide. It hit the ground and bounced, shedding a wheel, then slid to a halt the right way up two miles inside the British lines, close to some Australian trenches.

Not only Brown had fired at von Richthofen. Near Corbie, two Australians of the 24th Machine-Gun Company – Sergeant C. B. Popkin and Gunner R. F. Weston – had loosed off a long burst at the triplane as it flew low past them in pursuit of May. A few seconds later, two anti-aircraft Lewis guns of the 53rd Battery, 14th Australian Field Artillery Brigade, manned by Gunners W. J. Evans and R. Buie, had also fired on it. Later, all these men were to claim the credit for shooting down von Richthofen.

The triplane's heavy landing was witnessed by Sergeant-Major J. H. Sheridan of the 3rd Battery, Royal Artillery, who had been watching the chase. Sheridan waited for the German pilot to climb out, but when there was no movement the soldier ran forward and peered into the cockpit. The pilot was slumped forward, his head resting against the breech of one of his machine-guns. One hand still gripped the stick. Blood oozed from his mouth and from a hole in his chest where a bullet had made its exit, having traversed his body after entering the right side. There was no doubt that he was dead.

The following day, a British aircraft flew over the German airfield at Cappy and dropped a message. It read: 'To the German Flying Corps. Rittmeister Baron von Richthofen was killed in aerial combat on 21 April 1918. He was buried with full military honours. From the British Royal Air Force.'

Manfred von Richthofen's body was later removed to a German war cemetery, and in 1925 it was finally laid to rest in Berlin. Roy Brown flew several more missions before being sent home to England, where he was admitted to hospital suffering from severe stomach trouble and nervous strain. After the war he went back to Canada and became a businessman. He died in 1944 at the age of only fifty, having never fully recovered his health. Lieutenant W. R. May went on to score thirteen victories and win a Distinguished Flying Cross; he too went back to Canada, where he took up a career in civil aviation. He died in 1952.

Although Roy Brown was officially credited with the killing of von Richthofen, no one really knows to this day whose bullet sent him down. Except to adherents of the 'Red Baron cult' which has grown in recent years along with an upsurge of interest in First World War aviation, the fact of who killed him is relatively unimportant. What was important was the profound effect his death had on millions of Germans, soldiers and civilians alike. According to General Ludendorff, the psychological impact of his death was equivalent to the loss of thirty divisions. The Richthofen *Geschwader* continued to fight hard under new commanders, but the loss of von Richthofen's personal leadership was noticeable. For the German Flying Corps, it was as though that day in April 1918 marked the start of the slide into final defeat.

It almost marked the end of Ludendorff's aspirations on the Somme, too, although in April the Germans had made a desperate final effort to gain the upper hand by switching the focus of their attacks against the British 2nd Army, covering the Ypres–Armentières sector in the north, on the Lys, with the object of breaking through to the vital supply ports of Calais and Boulogne. The 2nd Army now included the remnants of the 5th; the British 1st Army lay to the south, on the right flank, with French forces separating the two along a few miles of the front.

The pattern of the German attack, and the ground-attack operations that accompanied it, were similar to those that had unfolded on the Somme, although in many ways the British situation on the Lys was more perilous. The few miles between the front and the Channel coast allowed no room for manoeuvre and the area was crammed with supply dumps and airfields, whose loss would have been immediately fatal. The first German objective was the railway junction before Hazebrouck, and at one time the enemy spearheads were within four miles of it. Only a stout resistance in the north, and a very gallant and costly stand by the 55th West Lancashire

Division at Givenchy, on the southern flank, prevented the total disintegration of the Allied Line.

Conditions on the Lys were different from those on the Somme. The countryside around the Lys was a maze of lanes, streams, canals and dykes, and flying conditions were more arduous. The March weather had given way to mist that hung heavily over the damp Flanders plain, and there were frequent squalls of snow and sleet. Nevertheless, the British air effort, although not as sustained as it had been during March, had its effect on the enemy, as extracts from the German war diaries for the mid-April period once again reveal.

'The battalions all suffered severely during their approach march from the British low flying aircraft which attacked them savagely with machine-gun fire and bombs . . . The attack did not take place . . . but the tired, worn-out troops, closely packed together, suffered heavily from the bombs and machine-guns of enemy aeroplanes . . . Everywhere I heard complaints about the heavy losses caused by bombing attacks, especially in horses which had no protection.'

The last were the words of General von Arnim, commanding the German 4th Army.

On 21 April, four weeks after they had begun under such terrible pressure, the great Allied retreats of spring 1918 ended, and by the end of the month the Allied lines were consolidating into strong trench systems. On the Somme, the last German attack was made on 24 April when they captured Villers Bretonneux and Hangard, but Australian troops retook these objectives the following night. The Germans had played their last card in a final bid to take Amiens, and they had lost.

CHAPTER FIVE

The German Flying Corps had failed to achieve the air superiority that was necessary to the success of their offensives of March and April 1918. Had the *Jagdgeschwader* been able to avail themselves, at the start of the Ludendorff Offensives, of the new combat aircraft that were at last beginning to reach the front-line units in late April, it might have been a different story.

The first of the new types was the Fokker D.VII, which had its origins late in 1917. At that time the German Flying Corps was beginning to lose the ascendancy it had enjoyed for nearly three years, as Allied air units became equipped with more modern aircraft such as the SPAD, SE5 and Camel. The German High Command considered the situation to be so serious that it ordered German aircraft manufacturers to develop new fighter types without delay. The various fighters would take part in a competitive fly-off at Johannisthal, and the winning firm would be awarded large production contracts for its design.

Anthony Fokker's contender, the D.VII fighter biplane, was completed in November 1917 in something of a hurry, as Fokker later described.

'The competition date arrived several days sooner than I found desirable. I was working day and night on the plane, but in order to be represented at all I had hurriedly to finish off a model considerably short of what I had in mind. It was a biplane and, in deference to conservatism, the wings were connected near the tips by single 'N' struts. The fuselage section I left square to facilitate manufacture. I retained the tiny aerofoil surface (which had characterized the D.VI and other Fokker scouts) which streamlined the landing gear axle, and the whole plane was designed around the coveted 160 hp Mercedes six-cylinder motor, for it was part of the competition rules that every entrant should use this engine – the only one available in quantity! With only just enough time to make a sketchy test hop at Schwerin to determine whether my plane would fly at all, we loaded it on a truck and raced to Johannisthal.'

Even the hasty trial had shown that the aircraft had an excellent all-round performance, but it was very sensitive, with tricky habits, and a tendency to spin on the slightest provocation. It was much too responsive on the controls, particularly in turns. The rules of the competition permitted manufacturers to demonstrate their entries either personally or with an official test pilot, and Fokker took advantage of this on the first few days to make a thorough investigation of the aircraft's faults. Subsequently, all manufacturers were to be barred from Johannisthal and the aircraft turned over to operational pilots for a comparison of their fighting qualities. The judges were the cream of Germany's fighter pilots.

Fokker, as it turned out, was the only manufacturer to fly his own aircraft.

'I flew each day, learning as much about the ship as possible, and showing by direct comparison that it would out-perform any other plane in the sky. Keeping it well in hand, watching its tricks, I played with the other pilots, diving on them, circling them, swooping in under their tails, looping around them, driving their planes down to earth and in general enjoying myself to the utmost while displaying my ship to best advantage. The manoeuvrability of my plane in short, sharp turns at low altitudes was particularly impressive. At the same time I began to realize that if one of the operational pilots took the ship up in its present form and endeavoured to emulate my performance, he would probably kill himself. Finally, I concluded that the fuselage lacked sufficient rear side area, had too much front side area, and that the fin and rudder were too small. Something had to be done for, on Monday, the planes were to be turned over to the operational pilots.

'That Saturday I telephoned Schwerin for two of my best welders to come at once. As soon as night fell we locked ourselves in the dim hangar to reconstruct the ship. In its cavernous depths we laboured like gnomes under the violet glare of acetylene torches, cutting through the fuselage to weld in another bay of two feet, and enlarging the fin in equal ratio. It was a long, exhausting job all through the night and lasting until Sunday noon. In the end the fabric was patched so smoothly that nothing appeared to have been done to the ship. Weary

68

though I was, I had yet to take my ship up once more to determine whether the alterations had remedied its faults. In the main they had. The fighter was no longer dangerous to its pilot, though it still swung around corners at a fast clip. Properly employed, this characteristic was an asset. The spinning tendency had disappeared . . . in the hands of an experienced pilot, aware of its weakness, that sensitivity of control became its strength.

'With a lighter heart I landed, and next day my plane was turned over to the Contest Committee. Before leaving the field for good, however, I sauntered over to a group of pilots who were waiting to test the various planes. I pulled *Oberleutnant* Bruno Loerzer, who commanded a front-line *Jagdstaffel*, on one side. 'You'll notice a special feature of my ship, *Herr Leutnant*,' I said, 'its quickness in turns. Let the others in on it so that they can show it off to best advantage.' Then I left, having put them on their guard without their realizing it, ostensibly to seek some much-needed sleep.

'With that little tip, they demonstrated the plane as well or better than I could have done myself. At altitude the plane's performance was particularly good because of the thick wing, and this factor was highly important.'

Fokker secretly took off from the other side of the airfield on an old experimental aircraft which he had planted there earlier and climbed to 15,000 feet to watch the fly-off.

'I was delighted with the manner in which the Fokker was showing up the others. None of my chief competitors, the Rumpler, the LFG, the Albatros or the Pfalz was in the running. The pilots, following Loerzer's tip-off, flew my ship in much the same way as I had done from the first day, playing with the other planes and out-manoeuvring them all the way down from 15,000 to 1,000 feet, displaying in every way the unmistakable superiority of the Fokker. The Rumpler was much faster and had a nice climb but suffered a rather high wing loading. It was my most dangerous competitor. The arrangement of the radiators on the fuselage sides, however, disturbed the airflow around the control surfaces so that it handled badly at awkward moments. Otherwise it was a clean ship and gave a good account of itself.'

By the fourth day of the fly-off it was clear that the Fokker was by far the best all-round design, and superior to the other prototypes in mock combat. At high altitude the Rumpler slipped away in turns, losing height rapidly while the Fokker stayed firmly under control; the Albatros DVI was almost a duplicate of the earlier DV and showed no improvement, the Pfalz showed dangerous structural weaknesses, the Roland-designed LFG had hardly any visibility from the cockpit, and the AEG contender was a hopeless failure on all counts.

Nevertheless, Fokker was staggered when Captain Falken-hein, adjutant to the German Flying Corps C-in-C, General von Hoeppner, asked him to name a price for building four hundred aircraft. Up to that time, the largest order Fokker had ever received for a fighter aircraft had been for sixty DRI triplanes. He told the officer that the total cost would be ten million marks. Falkenhein agreed without hesitation, and told Fokker that the Albatros factory was also to build the new aircraft on a royalty basis.

'Momentarily I was stunned,' Fokker admitted. 'Although all efforts had been directed towards staging a comeback, the thoroughness of it rather swept me off my feet. After nearly a year as the front-line favourite, the Albatros was scrapped and the Army was forcing the Albatros Werke to build my plane on a five per cent royalty basis. Soon the so-called Hindenburg Programme was to come into effect, calling for an enormous expansion of the air arm, and the AEG factory was also to be ordered to build my D.VII.'

Despite all the priority given to the production of the D.VII, it took time to set up the necessary machinery and it was not until the last days of April 1918 that the first examples were delivered to *Jagdgeschwader* 1, which was now commanded by Captain Wilhelm Reinhard. The new aircraft cost Reinhard his life, for he was accidentally killed while flying one a few days later. So JG 1 received its third and last commanding officer, a leader of proven worth who had twenty victories to his credit and who wore the *Pour le Mérite*: Lieutenant Hermann Goering.

Other German pilots, however, believed that the finest fighter at the front in the summer of 1918 came from a different stable. This was the Siemens-Schuckert D.III, a stubby, compact little biplane of wooden construction powered by a 160 hp Siemens-Halske rotary engine. During flight trials in October

1917, the prototype D.III had reached a level speed of 112 mph and climbed to 19,600 feet in less than twenty minutes, a performance good enough for it to be ordered into production. At the same time, the IDFLIEG – *Inspektion der Fliegertruppen* – placed orders for two further developments, the D.IV and D.V.

The first batch of thirty SSW D.III fighters were delivered for operational trials in January 1918, and in February the IDFLIEG ordered thirty more aircraft. Beginning in late April, forty-one examples were sent to the Western Front; most of them went to *Jagdgeschwader* 2, which equipped its *Jasta* 15 with the type. The pilots were delighted with the new aircraft, and a typical verdict on the SSW D.III was that it was highly sensitive on the controls, possessed excellent flying qualities and climbed like a rocket.

One German ace who firmly advocated the SSW D.III was Captain Rudolf Berthold, a talented pilot who had begun his combat career with *Fliegerabteilung* 23 in 1916, scoring his first victories while flying a Fokker Monoplane. He survived a series of close shaves – including a tricky forced landing after a fight with three BE2Cs and a crash while testing a Pfalz Scout – and in October 1916, while commanding *Jasta* 14, he scored his tenth victory and was awarded the *Pour le Mérite*. In August 1917 he assumed command of *Jasta* 18, and in one month he destroyed fourteen RFC aircraft before being shot down himself and severely wounded in the right arm.

Returning to action in the spring of 1918, he took command of *Jagdgeschwader* 2, comprising *Jastas* 12, 13, 15 and 19. When JG 2 received the Fokker D.VII, he had his aircraft specially modified so that he could fly and fight with his one good hand and the limited use of the other. He was in constant pain from his injury and his determination was greatly admired by his fellow pilots, who nicknamed him the 'Iron Knight'. His SSW D.III, which he tested in action during the first weeks of May 1918, was distinctively painted with a red and blue engine cowling and a flaming sword insignia.

Berthold's report on the aircraft, which he submitted to the IDFLIEG on 23 May, read:

'Basically the new Siemens-Halske Sh.III engine is sound and the pilots have faith in it. One particular advantage is that engine power

71

remains constant even at high altitude. After rectifying the defects reported to the Commanding General of the Air Service by *Jagdgeschwader* 2 on 17 April 1918, and particularly after reducing the control forces and the excessive left-hand torque suffered by the aircraft, the SSW D.III can be considered a perfectly acceptable front-line machine, but the aircraft cannot be used at the present time as, after seven to ten hours' running of the Sh.III engine the pistons seize, the crowns being torn off and the pieces dropping into the crankcase.'

Berthold went on to list the possible causes of this major defect, including inadequate engine cooling, inferior castor oil substitute and weakness in the alloy used for the pistons, and concluded: 'It is urgently required that this fighter be made available again for front-line use as quickly as possible, for after the elimination of its present faults it is likely to become one of our most successful fighter aircraft.'

As a result of Berthold's report, the thirty-five SSW D.IIIs were withdrawn from front-line service at the end of May and returned to the Siemens-Schuckert factory for airframe and engine modifications. It was to be two months before they returned to operational service, and then they were used mainly for home defence duties. *Jasta* 15 reverted to the Fokker D.VII, and it was while flying one of these, on 10 August 1918, that Rudolf Berthold scored his last two victories, bringing his final tally to forty-four. Soon afterwards, in a fight with Sopwith Camels, he was shot down and suffered yet more injuries. He survived them only to be murdered by German Communists in Harburg on 15 December 1919.

The French were among the first to encounter the new Fokker D.VII. On 6 May 1918, sixteen SPADs of Lieutenant Jean Chaput's SPA 57, operating in support of the 8th French Army on the Oise, encountered an equal number of D.VIIs. This time the French came out on top, claiming five Fokkers in a dogfight that left the pilots utterly exhausted. One by one they straggled back to base, but one pilot was missing. Troops in the French front line saw a SPAD spiral down and make a heavy landing in no-man's land. They rushed to drag the pilot from the wreck, but there was nothing they could do. Jean Chaput had three bullets in him, and he was dead. He had sixteen victories.

Three days later, Chaput's death was avenged by René Fonck, who equalled the record of RAF pilots John Trollope and Henry Woollett by shooting down six aircraft in a single day, three of them in the space of a minute. These were all two-seaters, which he caught flying in formation over Grivesnes. The first one went down before his guns at 4.05 pm, the next one ten seconds later, and the third after a forty-second running battle. He landed to refuel and have something to eat; then, on a second patrol, he sighted a formation of Pfalz Scouts and engaged them at 6.40, shooting down the first one almost immediately. He destroyed a second at 6.45, and another ten seconds later. The destruction of all six aircraft had cost him just fifty-two rounds of ammunition.

If May 1918 was René Fonck's month, the same was certainly true for Mick Mannock, whose No 74 Squadron was everywhere in the thick of the fighting. A glimpse at the official record for the month tells its own tale.

'*May 6th*. Captain E. Mannock . . . engaged one EA triplane and forced it into a spin. He followed the EA down, firing short bursts and the EA finally turned over on its back and crashed.

'*May 12th*. Captain E. Mannock, 74 Sqn, with his patrol, encountered a formation of eight EA scouts; he attacked the rear machine at close range and at right angles, and the EA side-slipped underneath him and collided with another enemy scout, both enemy machines falling to pieces in the air. Capt Mannock then engaged another EA scout from behind and fired a long burst into it from both guns; the EA went down vertically and was seen to dive into the ground.

'*May 16th*. Capt E. Mannock, 74 Sqn, fired about 40 rounds at one EA scout which went into a vertical dive and broke to pieces in the air.

'*May 17th*. Capt E. Mannock . . . attacked the rear machine of a formation of EA scouts and fired a long burst from both guns into it, and the EA spun down out of control. Capt Mannock was then attacked by another EA and forced to spin away, but 210 Squadron confirm the first EA attacked by Capt Mannock as having crashed in flames. Later in the day Capt Mannock observed an EA two-seater crossing the line near Ypres. He climbed north and then east and approached the EA at which he fired approximately 200 rounds at close range during a fight which lasted about one minute, the EA going down alternately diving and spinning. At about 4,000 feet the EA burst into flames and was seen to crash and to burn itself out on the ground.

'*May 18th*. Capt E. Mannock engaged an enemy two-seater at right-angles, firing a burst of 40 rounds into it. The EA went down in a vertical dive and crashed near Steenwerck, and burst into flames on hitting the ground.

'*May 21st*. A patrol of 74 Squadron encountered six Pfalz Scouts, upon whom they dived, shooting down five of them – of which Major K. L. Caldwell destroyed one, Captain E. Mannock three, and Captain W. E. Young one. Captain Mannock also destroyed another EA earlier in the day.'

Mannock's young pilots were justifiably proud of their leader's prowess in action. One of them, Lieutenant Ira 'Taffy' Jones, who himself was to destroy forty enemy aircraft before the war's end, noted in his diary on 25 May:

'The CO saved Giles' skin today. Giles very carelessly allowed a black Albatros to pounce on him while he was concentrating on the destruction of a silver-grey two-seater. Giles has had his leg pulled unmercifully; we declare he was decoyed. Pilots hate admitting that they have been taken in as a sucker!

'Clements tells me that Mick saved his life tonight, too. Mick and Clements went up for a bit of fun after tea. They each got what they wanted . . . Clements spotted a large formation of Huns obviously making a beeline for them. Clements put on full throttle . . . to catch up to Mick, who as usual was wasting no time in getting at his enemy. Mick had seen the Hun formation all the time . . . he turned west quickly and dived, the Huns following and firing. Mick saved Clements by losing height directly beneath them and so drawing them on to him, while Clements got clear. Clements says it was a rotten sight to see one SE being attacked by such a bunch, and that had it been anyone except Mick, he would have been anxious about his safety. (We all believe that no Hun will ever shoot down Mick.) One Pfalz followed him very closely, and suddenly Mick went down out of control; on his back – spinning – and doing everything imaginable from 8,000 to 4,000 feet. At 5,000 feet the Hun, completely fooled, flattened out to watch the crash. Mick then decided he had had enough, and flattened out too and made for our lines – diving hard.'

Four days later, on 29 May, Jones wrote:

'Mick took Clements and me up at 7.00 pm . . . Mick spotted about a dozen Huns coming from the direction of Roubaix; we were then over Lille. As we had not too much time for a fight, having already been up for over an hour, he decided to go straight at them, as we had a slight advantage of height. The Huns, who were Albatros Scouts, were of the stout variety, and they accepted our challenge. Both Mick and the Hun leader opened fire at one another as they approached from about 300 yards' range, but nothing happened. This burst of fire was the signal for a glorious dogfight – as fine and as frightening a dogfight as I've ever been in. Friend and foe fired at and whistled past one another at a tornado pace . . . I have never been so frightened in my life. Of late I have been able to keep very cool during the actual fight, but tonight I became so flustered that occasionally I fired at my own pals in an effort not to miss a chance – thank God, my shooting was erratic. How terrible it would have been if I had, say, shot Mick down! The thought gives me the very creeps . . . Mick sent two slate-blue Albatros down out of control, and Clements crashed his first Hun. He is very bucked about it. It is wonderful how cheered a pilot becomes after he shoots down his first machine – his morale increases by at least a hundred per cent. This is why Mick gives Huns away – to raise the morale of the beginner.'

Taffy Jones himself destroyed his first enemy aircraft on 8 May and ran up a steady score during the remainder of the month. He drove an Albatros down out of control the next day, and on the 17th, with his patrol, attacked ten Pfalz Scouts. During the battle he saw a two-seater slightly in front and just below him, and opened up with both guns. He saw hits on the engine and both cockpits and the enemy went down vertically, trailing smoke and eventually bursting into flames, to crash

75

near Estaires. On the following day he attacked another two-seater, which was being engaged by anti-aircraft fire at the time, and fired 250 rounds into it from underneath its tail. There was an explosion and the enemy aircraft caught fire and crashed. More anti-aircraft bursts led him to another two-seater over Hazebrouck; he attacked this aircraft too from below but ran into heavy defensive fire from its observer, who was shooting through a hole in the fuselage floor. Jones described what happened then:

'Very suddenly he tilted his machine very steeply, and it seemed as if a black object had been deliberately thrown at me. I thought at first it was the observer's gun, so I slithered quickly to the other side and as I did so, looked for the object. To my amazement, I saw the body of the observer, falling with arms outstretched and legs wide apart, and going down in a series of tumbling circles. It was a horrifying sight. He fell in the trenches near Meteren.'

Jones turned back to engage the two-seater, which was heading east at high speed, but a shortage of ammunition and a gun jam compelled him to break off the action and the enemy got away. A Pfalz Scout which he engaged on 22 May was not so lucky; its wings broke off and the fuselage went down like a bomb to explode on impact.

Another leading pilot who added to his score during the hectic air fighting of May 1918 was Captain A. W. Beauchamp-Proctor of No 84 Squadron (SE5as), a South African who was to end the war as the fifth-ranking RAF ace with fifty-four victories. On 10 May Beauchamp-Proctor stalked a two-seater which he had sighted climbing for altitude before crossing the British lines and fired fifty rounds into it, killing the observer. He then closed right in and opened fire again, at which the two-seater went into a vertical dive. The RAF pilot watched it fall through 4,000 feet until he lost it in the haze, but it was confirmed as having crashed by another 84 Squadron pilot.

Five days later, Beauchamp-Proctor took off from No 84 Squadron's airfield at Bertangles in the darkness before dawn to intercept enemy bombers that had been attacking Amiens. He failed to find them, so flew east in the hope of catching them over their airfield as they returned from the bombing mission. Landing flares led him to the enemy aerodrome; he throttled back and glided down to 3,000 feet, then circled a few miles west of the enemy field to await events. A few minutes later a twin-engined aircraft – probably a Gotha – flew just over him and he turned to intercept, but its gunner was on the alert and opened up. Proctor fired a long burst and the enemy gunner fell silent. Proctor's own gun then jammed, and by the time he had cleared the stoppage the enemy aircraft was almost over the airfield. He opened fire again and saw the enemy machine shoot off a red flare, which was answered from the ground. The next instant all hell broke loose and Proctor found himself flying through a storm of heavy machine-gun fire and tracer shells. He was forced to break off the combat at 2,000 feet, having driven the enemy aircraft some distance away from its aerodrome. He later reported that it was in a dive when he last saw it, and although it was still probably under control it had almost certainly suffered heavy damage.

It was the Canadian, Captain D. M. MacLaren of No 46 Squadron (Sopwith Camel), who was to share joint fifth place with Beauchamp-Proctor at the end of hostilities. MacLaren's first success in May came on the 3rd, when he fired 75 rounds into a two-seater from a range of fifty yards and sent it down in flames. Almost immediately afterwards he shared in the destruction of a second two-seater with another 46 Squadron pilot, 2nd Lieutenant V. M. Yeates.

On 6 May MacLaren, together with Yeates and three other 46 Squadron pilots, harried another two-seater to destruction, and in that same week MacLaren drove two more enemy machines down out of control, but was unable to confirm them as positive victories. A few days later he shared another with Lieutenant C. R. Chapman, and on 20 May he shot down two enemy observation balloons in flames.

Major Roderic Dallas of No 40 Squadron entered May's air combats in determined fashion by shooting down a Pfalz Scout on the morning of the 2nd. Later in the day, he took his SE5 to the enemy airfield at La Brayelle and attacked it at low level, strafing the hangars. Ignoring desultory fire from the ground, he turned and flew back over the aerodrome to drop a parcel. In it was a pair of army boots and an accompanying message which read: 'If you won't come up here and fight, herewith one

pair of boots for work on the ground. Pilots – for the use of.'
Circling in the haze, he waited until a party of Germans had
gathered to examine the parcel and then made another low-
level run, firing 100 rounds of ammunition and dropping two
Cooper bombs on their heads. To complete his day's work, he
caught an Albatros Scout on his way home and sent it down in
flames.

Dallas destroyed two more enemy aircraft in mid-May, and
another on the 27th. It was his thirty-ninth and last victory,
although some sources put his score at fifty-one. His SE5,
always in the thick of the fighting, was well known to the
enemy; instead of the drab khaki upper surfaces and cream
underside that was the standard British colour scheme, he had
it painted in a distinctive green and brown pattern resembling
that which the RAF was to adopt many years later.

On 1 June 1918 Dallas set out on another of his lone patrols,
intending to lurk up-sun over the front line and trap an
unsuspecting enemy observation aircraft. He never returned.
Later, his wrecked aircraft was found near the village of Lieven.
A German account later told the story of Dallas's last minutes.
It appeared that he had dived down to attack a solitary Fokker
Triplane, unaware that two more were cruising several thousand feet higher up, waiting for just this moment. They
pounced on him and the SE went down, its pilot riddled with a
score of bullets.

Captain R. A. Little of No 203 Squadron also scored his last
victory in May. On the 22nd, having been forced to leave his
patrol because of oil pressure trouble, he was on his way home
when he encountered an Albatros CV two-seater. He attacked
it at close range and sent it down at St Leger, watching it crash
into a railway cutting.

The next day, the Australian pilot was shot down and killed
in the course of an offensive patrol. He had forty-seven
victories to his credit.

Other leading RAF scorers in May were Major James
Gilmour of No 65 Squadron (Sopwith Camel) and Lieutenant
A. C. Atkey of No 22 Squadron (Bristol Fighter). Gilmour
destroyed a pair of two-seaters on 2 May, and on the 9th he
shot down another and damaged a fourth. On the next day he
and his patrol caught a lone Albatros Scout and shared in

78

sending it down, and on 18 May he led his patrol into an attack on twelve enemy fighters, causing one to break up with his first burst of fire. Soon afterwards he dived on a two-seater and fired a long burst into it; it turned away eastwards and went into a long dive, then crashed and burst into flames on the ground.

Atkey, who had previously flown DH4s with No 18 Squadron and who had been awarded an MC in April, was posted to No 22 Squadron at the end of the month and teamed up with Lieutenant C. G. Gass as his observer. A formidable team they proved to be, as an air battle of 7 May showed. That morning, Atkey and Gass were in one of a pair of Bristol Fighters patrolling in showery weather when they ran into a formation of seven Albatros and Pfalz Scouts in the vicinity of Henin-Liétard. The two Bristols – the second aircraft was crewed by Lieutenants J. E. Gurdon and A. J. H. Thornton – immediately went into the attack and soon found themselves in the middle of a fierce fight, for the original enemy formation was quickly reinforced by two others which brought the number of enemy aircraft involved to twenty. Of all battles, this one proved conclusively that the Bristol Fighter, in expert hands, could more than hold its own against a far superior enemy force. During a dogfight that lasted half an hour, Atkey and Gass shot down two enemy aircraft in flames and saw three more crash, while Gurdon and Thornton disposed of three more, two of them in flames. The remainder did not stay to fight.

Two days later, the same team of Atkey and Gass destroyed another enemy scout, and on a second patrol that day they carried out a single-handed attack on a formation of eight enemy machines, Atkey firing fifty rounds into one at close range. Flames burst from the fuselage behind the pilot's seat and it went down to crash. Later in the week they drove three more enemy aircraft down out of control – which, in the parlance of the First World War, meant that they were probably destroyed – and on 19 May they shot down a two-seater near Douai. During the next few days they drove four more Germans down out of control, and rounded off the month with a spirited engagement on the 25th. The official record tersely tells the story:

'A patrol of 22 Squadron, led by Captain A. C. Atkey and 2nd Lt C. G. Gass, while escorting DH4s of 18 Sqn, encountered a large formation of about 40 EA. A fierce fight ensued, in the course of which so many EA were seen spinning and diving away that it was impossible to tell whether they were out of control or not. At the conclusion of the fight four EA were seen crashed on the ground, and in addition, one Albatros Scout, attacked by Lt S. F. H. Thompson and Sgt R. M. Fletcher, was seen to go down in flames.'

During May, the German Flying Corps did what it ought to have done during the crucial weeks of March and April: it launched a determined bombing campaign with the object of disrupting the British lines of communication, which were now heavily congested as a result of the earlier retreats. On the night of 19/20 May, fifteen Gothas attacked a vital railway bridge at Etaples over the Canche Estuary. They failed to hit the target, but their bombs fell on a nearby military hospital, killing 182 patients and injuring 643. The crew of one of the bombers, which had to make a forced landing after being hit by anti-aircraft fire, expressed incredulity that the British authorities had placed a hospital so close to a vital military objective, maintaining that they had no prior knowledge of the hospital's whereabouts. There is no reason to doubt their claim. On the last night of the month the German bombers had better success against their assigned target, destroying one span of the bridge.

The bombers' real success, however, was against the British ammunition and supply dumps. On 19/20 May, in conjunction with the Etaples raid, Gothas dropped some 500 bombs on No 12 Ordnance Depot at Blarges, which contained 27,000 tons of explosive. In all, 6,000 tons were destroyed. One dump containing mortar bombs received a direct hit and simply vanished, leaving a crater fifty yards wide and ten deep. On the next night the bombers attacked No 20 Ordnance Depot at Seigneville, wiping out 5,600 tons of ammunition including 69 million small-arms rounds. Now the Allied line in the north was stabilizing, these losses were severe, though not critical. Had they occurred a few weeks earlier, with the field commanders crying out for supplies of ammunition and equipment to sustain their battered and retreating armies, they would almost certainly have been disastrous.

Some British divisions, which had suffered particularly severe losses in the spring fighting, had been sent south to rest and recuperate on the Aisne. They were accompanied by a single RAF squadron, No 52, with RE8s. On 22 May the squadron's crews reported large clouds of dust swirling over the roads in the German rear areas, a sure sign of large-scale troop movement. They reported the same phenomenon the next day, and the day after that. The British commander in the area brought the RAF reports to the notice of the French general commanding the 6th Army, under whose orders he was serving, but the general took no notice.

Soon after midnight on 27 May, one of the heaviest bombardments of the war thundered down on the luckless British divisions. Two were virtually wiped out and a third suffered heavy losses. The fourth British division, in reserve, remained intact and was thrown into the battle, together with French reserves. By the time the German advance was halted it had penetrated the Allied front to a depth of twelve miles and had reached the Marne. The disaster prompted a stern reminder from the RAF C-in-C, Major-General Salmond, who ordered that in future every likely approach route was to be reconnoitred twice nightly and again just before dawn, the pilots flying at low level. 'The responsibility that the British Army is not surprised,' said Salmond, 'is on the Royal Air Force.'

Never again, in this war, would British troops in the field suffer through lack of adequate air reconnaissance; and never again would an Allied field commander fail to act upon the information supplied by the crews of the observation aircraft who daily risked their lives over enemy territory.

CHAPTER SIX

In the spring of 1918, after a lengthy period of training, the pilots of the American First Pursuit Group, comprising the 94th and 95th Squadrons, at last began to make their mark in the air fighting over the Western Front. The 94th Squadron, under Major Raoul Lufbery, was the first to be declared combat-ready, but Lufbery had fought a hard battle to bring it to this level; in the middle of April the Squadron's Nieuports still had no guns. It seemed that some supply officer, somewhere far to the rear, deemed the issue of socks more important than the issue of weapons. In the end Lufbery took his case directly to General Pershing, and after that guns arrived in record time.

On 18 April, three Nieuport Scouts of the 94th Aero Squadron were detailed to carry out the First Pursuit Group's first combat patrol. It was led by Captain David Petersen, with Lieutenants Reed Chambers and Edward Rickenbacker as his wingmen. The patrol was uneventful and the three pilots returned to their airfield, which was in the Champagne sector. Soon after they had landed, however, two German aircraft were reported in the area. Two more American pilots, Lieutenants Alan Winslow and Douglas Campbell, immediately took off and each shot down an enemy machine – the first air victories credited to an American squadron.

Lufbery's training schedule was not confined to work in the air. He was always available whenever his pilots wanted his advice, and he would spend long hours with them in the evenings, discussing tactics. His method of fighting was much the same as Mannock's; approach with caution and make sure the odds are in your favour before committing yourself. Above all, he told them, keep a cool head. Panic was the fighter pilot's worst enemy. If your aircraft is set on fire, he advised them, side-slip to keep the flames away from the cockpit and get down as quickly as you can. That way, you have at least some chance of survival; you have none at all if you panic and jump clear.

Raoul Lufbery's luck finally ran out on 19 May 1918, five weeks after he had scored his seventeenth and final victory: an Albatros DIII, which he shot down on a freelance patrol. During a fight with another Albatros right over the 94th Squadron's airfield at Toul, his Nieuport was hit and set on fire. In full view of the horrified Americans on the ground, it nosed down and was soon enveloped in flames. It was not hard to imagine the agony of the man in the cockpit as he tried to side-slip through the last few hundred feet. Finally, at only 200 feet above the ground, the flames won. The witnesses saw a dark shape detach itself and plummet to the ground.

They found Lufbery's body in a garden, impaled on a fence in the hamlet of Maron. It was thought that he may have been trying to jump into a small river, which flowed a hundred yards or so away. He was buried in a nearby military cemetery, but his body was later removed and laid to rest in the Parc de Garches, near Marnes-la-Coquette, where there stands a monument to the *Escadrille Lafayette* and its dead.

Although most of the American pilots gradually re-mustered into the US squadrons, some elected to stay with the French and the RAF. Foremost among the latter were Captain W. C. Lambert of No 24 Squadron, who was to end the war with twenty-two victories, Captain A. T. Iaccaci of No 20 Squadron (eighteen victories), Lieutenant F. W. Gillet of No 79 Squadron (seventeen victories), Captain H. A. Kuhlberg of No 1 Squadron and Captain O. J. Rose of No 92 Squadron (sixteen victories each). In addition, two all-American squadrons, the 17th and 148th, were formed in the summer of 1918 and remained part of the RAF for the duration of the war.

The leading scorer among the American pilots who elected to stay with the French Aviation Militaire was Sous-Lieutenant Frank Baylies. Born in New Bedford, Massachusetts, in September 1895, Baylies was one of the band of American citizens who had found his way into the war through enlisting in the Ambulance Service in 1916. His first combat unit was SPA 73, after which he was transferred to SPA 3 of GC 12 *Cigognes*. He scored his first victory with this unit, as a corporal, on 19 February 1918. He gained two more victories in March, two in April and seven in May. He quickly showed himself to be a daring and fearless pilot who was quite willing to take on an enemy squadron single-handed. The American Army offered him a transfer with the rank of captain but he refused, preferring to remain as a sergeant with the *Cigognes*.

Baylies had a very narrow escape on 28 March, when an enemy shell struck his aircraft as he was flying at 300 feet four miles behind the German lines. He kept his machine in the air long enough to reach no-man's land and then ran for it, narrowly avoiding capture by German troops who set off in hot pursuit. His luck held until 17 June, when he set out on patrol with two other NCO pilots. They encountered a formation of aircraft which they believed to be Sopwith Camels; it was a fatal error, for they were in fact Fokker D.VIIs. After a short battle, Baylies fell in flames behind the enemy lines at Crève-coeur-Lassigny; his fellow pilots escaped by the skin of their teeth, their aircraft riddled with holes. Like Lufbery, Baylies was eventually interred at the Lafayette Memorial. His final score was twelve enemy aircraft destroyed, all between 19 February and 31 May 1918.

Two other notable Americans who remained with the Aviation Militaire were James A. Connely and Edwin Parsons, both of whom survived the war with eight confirmed victories. Not a great deal is known about Connely except that he was born in Philadelphia and joined the French Army by way of the Foreign Legion; his flying service was with SPA 157 and SPA 163, and his victories were gained between April and November 1918. He died in New York in 1944.

Lieutenant Edwin C. Parsons is better documented. Born in 1892 at Holyokeh, Massachusetts, he joined the Ambulance Service in France in 1915 and obtained his pilot's brevet a year later. He joined SPA 3 in April 1918 and remained with this unit for the duration of the war, gaining his first victory on 4 September and his eighth on 1 October. In 1940, with the rank of Lieutenant-Commander, he was an instructor at the US Naval Air Station Pensacola, Florida, and subsequently served on board an aircraft carrier in the Solomons. He retired with the rank of Rear-Admiral, USN; his decorations included the *Croix de Guerre* with eight palm leaves, and he was made an Officer of the Legion of Honour in 1961. He died in May 1968 and is buried at Arlington National Cemetery, Washington.

At least one Englishman served with the Aviation Militaire.

Lieutenant Robert Waddington was born in Lyon in 1893, and appears still to have been a British citizen when he enlisted in the French Army. In March 1915 he was a machine-gunner with the 141st Infantry Regiment at Verdun, after which he transferred to flying duties and became a sergeant air gunner with *Escadrille* N67, equipped with Nieuport 12C two-seaters. Moving to SPA 12, he shot down his first enemy aircraft on 11 May 1917, having gained his pilot's brevet the previous year, and went on to score a further eleven victories with SPA 31 and SPA 154 before the end of hostilities. His decorations included the French, Belgian and Serbian *Croix de Guerre*, and he was made a Chevalier of the Legion of Honour. He returned to the *Armée de l'Air* as a lieutenant-colonel in 1939 and was appointed commandant of the fighter training school at Chartres, where he was wounded in a German bombing attack in May 1940. He was still living in France, in his nineties, in 1986.

For the Allied squadrons, late May and early June 1918 was a hectic period. Of the 1,232 first-line aircraft on the British inventory in France at the start of the Ludendorff Offensive on 21 March, 1,000 were destroyed during the four weeks that followed. The total included 195 missing, 695 wrecked and 141 burnt or abandoned as their aerodromes were threatened by the German advance. On the credit side, the RFC/RAF had claimed 354 enemy aircraft shot down and 188 driven down out of control; with French claims, which are uncertain, added to this, the losses of both sides were probably about equal.

To make good the RAF losses, fresh squadrons were sent out from England. One of them was No 85, equipped with SE5as, which arrived at Petite Synthe on 25 May. Its commanding officer was Major W. A. Bishop VC, whose score at that time stood at sixty enemy aircraft destroyed.

Billy Bishop reopened his scoring on 27 May, when he attacked an enemy two-seater over Houthulst Forest. He chased it, firing as it turned east, and saw both sets of wings break off, followed by the tail unit. The fragments crashed east of Passchendaele. On the 30th he shot down two more two-seaters, and accounted for an Albatros Scout later in the day. Then came the blow: on 3 June the RAF C-in-C, Brigadier-General Salmond, decided that Bishop was too valuable an asset as a leader to have his life continually at risk, and ordered him to return to England in a fortnight's time.

During that fortnight, Bishop flew and fought as never before. In a period of twelve days when the weather was fit for flying he destroyed a further twenty-five enemy aircraft, the first on 4 June. On 17 June, his last day in action but one, he shot down three in the space of thirty minutes with the expenditure of only fifty-five rounds of ammunition. His combat report describes the action:

'*10.25 am. Staden and Hooglede. 18,000 feet.*
(1) Between Staden and Hooglede, 18,000 feet at 10.25 am, I turned back a two-seater who was approaching our lines, finally closing to seventy-five yards. After twenty rounds he burst into flames.

'*10.50 am. Sailly-sur-Lys. 4,000 feet.*
(2) Over Sailly-sur-Lys, 4,000 feet at 10.50 am, seeing one Albatros I zoomed into the edge of a cloud. Albatros passed cloud and I secured position on tail. After fifteen rounds he fell and crashed just south of village.

'*10.55 am. Laventie (near). 2,000 feet.*
(3) After attacking (2) I saw a two-seater EA quite low. I dived at him from the east but he turned and got east of me. After second burst of twenty rounds he fell in a turning dive, then crashed between Laventie and the main road.'

The next day, his last, was even more dramatic. Patrolling near Ypres, he saw and attacked three Pfalz fighters, one of which he quickly sent down in flames. As the others turned to attack him, two more Pfalz dropped down from the clouds to join the fray. For a few minutes the five machines circled, the Germans waiting for a chance to get in a killing burst. Then, as two of the Pfalz turned towards him, Bishop acted quickly. He dived between them and the two enemy aircraft, tightening their turns, collided with one another and fluttered down in a cloud of wreckage. The other two immediately broke and fled; Bishop went after them, opening fire on one from 200 yards. The Pfalz went down and burst into flames. The sole survivor, to Bishop's annoyance, escaped into a cloud.

The next day, Bishop left France for good. In just over a year

1. Members of *Jagdegeschwader* 1 pose beside an Albatross D.III in 1917. Manfred von Richthofen is in the cockpit and his brother Lothar is seated in the foreground. The youthful figure directly below von Richthofen is Hermann Goering, who was destined to become JG1's last commander.
2. Rittmeister Freiherr Manfred von Richthofen.
3. Lieutenant Arthur Rhys-Davids, the man who shot down Werner Voss. Rhys-Davids was himself shot down and killed only a few weeks later.

4. Major W. A. 'Billy' Bishop, VC, the top-scoring surviving British ace with 72 victories.
5. Captain Georges Guynemer, the hero of the French nation in 1917. He was shot down and killed in September of that year.
6. Captain René Fonck, the French ace of aces who ended the war with 75 victories. He died in Paris in 1953 at the age of 59, an embittered man through his treatment by the French people at the end of World War Two.
7. Major Edward 'Mick' Mannock, VC. With 73 victories Mannock was the top-scoring British ace, but was shot down and killed in 1918.

8. Major Raymond Collishaw, the ace who specialised in attacks on air-fields. During WW2 he was instrumental in helping to form the RAF's Desert Air Force.

9. Lieutenant Charles Nungesser, who might have become France's top-scoring pilot had it not been for physical disabilities caused by the strain of combat. In 1927, he vanished without trace in a bid to fly the Atlantic.

10. Pilots and observers of No. 22 Squadron, RAF, pictured on 1 April 1918, the day the RAF came into being. They were too busy fighting to take much notice of the occasion.

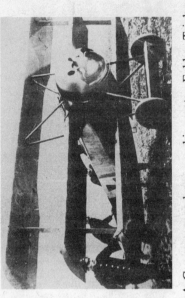

11. An RE8 observation aircraft, widely used by the RAF's Corps squadrons. The 'Harry Tate' suffered heavy losses, but performed its task well.
12. The Armstrong-Whitworth FK8 was more robust than the RE8 and could usually give a better account of itself in action.

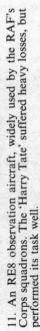

13. A German ground crew pushing out a Fokker Triplane prior to take-off. This type was favoured by the leading German aces until the arrival of the Fokker D.VII.
14. The nimble Fokker D.VII might have turned the air war in the Germans' favour had it been in service during the Ludendorff Offensive of March 1918.

15. Tricky to fly, the Sopwith Camel was a fine fighting machine in the hands of an experienced pilot, and destroyed more enemy aircraft than any other Allied type.

16. It was a Camel, flown by Captain Roy Brown, that reportedly shot down von Richthofen – although doubt remains to this day as to who should have the credit. Here, pilots of No 209 Squadron examine the guns from Richthofen's Triplane.

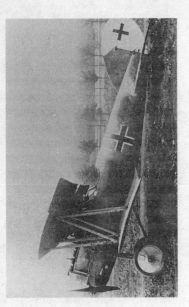

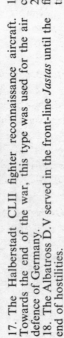

17. The Halberstadt CLII fighter reconnaissance aircraft. Towards the end of the war, this type was used for the air defence of Germany.
18. The Albatross D.V served in the front-line Jastas until the end of hostilities.

19. The Pfalz D.XII fighter. Most Jastas included a few aircraft of this type on their strength.
20. The Siemens-Schuckert SSW D.IV. Reputedly the finest fighter of World War One, it was beset by early technical troubles and entered service too late to influence the course of the air war.

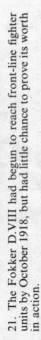

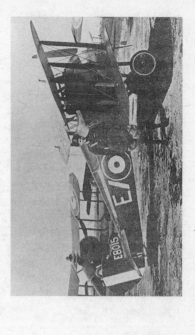

21. The Fokker D.VIII had begun to reach front-line fighter units by October 1918, but had little chance to prove its worth in action.

22. The SE5, flown by many leading British aces, was held by many to be the 'Spitfire' of the First World War.

23. The Bristol Fighter, after suffering early losses, proved to be a superlative fighting machine when its crews adopted the right tactics.

24. Sopwith Snipes of No 43 Squadron, the unit that first equipped with the type in August 1918.

25. Major W. G. 'Bill' Barker VC. While flying a Snipe on 27 October 1918, Barker fought an heroic single-handed battle against some fifty enemy aircraft.

26. The DH9 was designed to succeed the DH4, but its performance was little better. The DH9 day bomber squadrons suffered appalling losses, many through engine failures.

of air combat he had sent seventy-two enemy aircraft to destruction. In this top-scoring bracket, only he and one other pilot – the Frenchman, René Fonck – were destined to survive the war.

During the Second World War, Billy Bishop – now an Air Marshal – was placed in charge of recruiting for the Royal Canadian Air Force. For this work he received the CB to add to his already impressive list of decorations. He died of an illness on 11 September 1956.

Another leading pilot who came back into action during this period was Major Raymond Collishaw of No 203 Squadron, who celebrated his return in the second week of June by shooting down two enemy aircraft, and claimed another a few days later. However, his return coincided with the onset of poor weather, and he was unable to increase his tally before the end of the month. As before, Collishaw's forte was low-level airfield attacks, as we shall see later.

No 74 Squadron got away to a good start in June, three of its pilots – Mannock, Jones and Clements – destroying eight enemy aircraft between them in the first week. Mannock's three victories were all gained on 1 June in ten minutes and the victims were Pfalz Scouts which he described as 'dark camouflaged with white tails'.

'Observed and engaged formation of EA scouts east of Merville. Attacked from the front and above. The highest scout being behind, SE opened fire with both guns at point-blank range. The EA's bottom wings fell off and it crashed. Confirmed also by Lts Giles and Birch.

'Engaged another EA and after a short vertical burst at close range, this scout burst into flames. Confirmed by all other members of patrol.

'Engaged another EA, which was turning towards me on the same level. Fired several short bursts at this machine whilst circling. The EA went into a spin, and disappeared from the fight.'

There is little doubt that, by this time, Mick Mannock was suffering from what would later be termed combat fatigue. He displayed all the classic symptoms: sudden rages, bouts of depression, irrational risk-taking. The recurring depression was reflected in a letter to his sister, written early in June 1918:

'Things are getting a bit intense just lately and I don't quite know how long my nerves will last out. I am rather old now, as airmen go,

87

for fighting. Still, one hopes for the best . . . These times are so horrible that occasionally I feel that life is not worth hanging on to myself . . . I am supposed to be going on leave on the nineteenth of this month (if I live long enough) and I shall call at Birmingham to see you all.'

Mannock did live long enough to go on leave, and in so doing he bade farewell to his beloved No 74 Squadron. On his return, he was to be promoted and given command of No 85 Squadron in place of Billy Bishop.

During the first week of June 1918, the RAF claimed the destruction of fifty-six enemy aircraft over the Western Front, with a further twenty-six 'driven down out of control'. These figures are almost certainly greatly exaggerated, as have been all air combat claims since. There is, however, no doubt about the twelve RAF aircraft that failed to return during the week, a relatively low figure that speaks for the lack of air activity on most days. The previous week's figure was twenty-five, and the following week it went up to thirty-one as the German fighters once again swarmed over the Somme.

During this second week the RAF claimed sixty-three enemy aircraft destroyed and thirty-one driven down, and not all of them fell to the guns of SEs and Camels. On 10 June, for example, Captain George Fox-Rule and Lieutenant E. H. Tredcroft of No 49 Squadron, Fourneuil, were carrying out a low-level bombing attack in their DH4 when they were jumped by five Albatros Scouts which cut off their line of escape. Fox-Rule promptly dived through the middle of the enemy formation and fired a long burst into the leader, which burst into flames and was seen to hit the ground. The DH4 was then attacked by three more enemy fighters, which came in from astern. Tredcroft opened fire, sending one down out of control and forcing the others to break off. Fox-Rule brought his aircraft safely back, although its tailplane bracing wires had been shot through.

In another incident on the same day, Lieutenant C. W. Peckham and Sergeant J. Grant of No 57 Squadron were carrying out a daylight bombing attack on an enemy ammunition dump at Bapaume when they were attacked by eight Fokker Triplanes. Grant fired at the first one, which went down in flames. The others then positioned themselves west of the DH4, forcing Peckham to fly north; one of them broke away and opened fire from beneath the bomber, but Peckham turned swiftly and dived on his attacker, firing eighty rounds into it from his front gun. It, too, went down in flames and the rest broke off the action, enabling the DH4 to make its escape.

Among June's noteworthy incidents was a gallant rescue attempt which, unfortunately, went amiss. On the 13th, Captain J. D. Belgrave, together with Lieutenants H. A. Gordon and R. G. Lewis of No 60 Squadron attacked an enemy two-seater which they sent down, apparently out of control. As Belgrave followed it down into the mist to make sure of it, Gordon noticed that Lewis was losing height, having apparently suffered damage. A few minutes later Lewis landed in enemy territory between Albaincourt and Chaulnes, smashing his undercarriage as he did so. Gordon landed successfully close by just as some German soldiers appeared on the scene and started to open fire on the stranded aircraft. Gordon jumped from the cockpit and ran over to his colleague's SE5, shouting at him to get clear and come across to the serviceable aircraft so that he could take off with both of them on board, but he was too late; Lewis was strolling towards the enemy soldiers, apparently oblivious to the fact that they were still shooting and possibly mistaking them for friendly troops. Gordon ran back to his own aircraft and took off, still under fire. He circled the spot and lined up on the body of German troops, intending to fire at them, but then he noticed that Lewis was standing among them and he did not shoot. Gordon flew back to his base with one wire of his rudder control shot through and a longeron almost shot away.

Four days later, on 17 June, the crew of a No 205 Squadron DH4 from Bois de Roche had a very lucky escape when, during a bombing attack on Chaulnes, the pilot – Captain Gamon – was hit in the head by shrapnel from an anti-aircraft burst, and fainted. More shrapnel struck the engine, severing the main fuel pipe, and a fire broke out. The DH4 went out of control and spiralled down for 1,000 feet; the fire went out and the observer, Major Goble, managed to bring the aircraft under control; he released his bombs and turned towards the lines, the DH4 gliding over them at 6,000 feet. At this point the pilot regained consciousness and took control again, just in time to take evasive action and shake off a Pfalz Scout which made several determined attacks on the aircraft. He landed safely a few minutes later.

Even more fortunate was a Lieutenant Smith of No 29 Balloon Section who, accompanied by Flight Sergeant Shepherd, was spotting for British artillery when their balloon was attacked by an enemy aircraft and set on fire. Both took to their parachutes – with which balloon observers, unlike the unfortunate RAF aircrews, were equipped – but Smith's failed to open. He fell for several hundred feet, crashed through the branches of a tree and fell into a bog, from which he emerged none the worse except for a shaking.

The failure to issue parachutes to flying personnel caused much unnecessary suffering and loss of life. In the early days, primitive parachutes were bulky and heavy, and to wear them would have imposed an unacceptable weight penalty, as well as restricting the pilot's movements. But by 1918, more powerful engines and improved parachute design had done away with such objections, and the RAF's doctrine that the wearing of parachutes would be detrimental to the aggressive spirit of its pilots was frankly nonsensical; exactly the opposite would have been true. The Germans, suffering increasingly heavy losses in action and anxious to conserve their remaining pool of pilots and observers, began to issue parachutes in the summer of 1918, to their allies as well as to their own personnel.

The bitterness and frustration felt by many RAF pilots over the lack of parachutes was summed up by Lieutenant Ira Jones of No 74 Squadron, writing of the air battle on 1 June when Mannock destroyed three enemy machines.

'For ten minutes the ten SEs engaged the seven Pfalz; and when the battle ended one enemy had gone down in flames, one had crashed, and one had gone out of control – all to Mick's guns – while we had lost our flight commander (Captain W. J. Cairns). A determined Pfalz got to within 25 yards of him and gave him the gun. His right wing was suddenly seen to break up, the nose of his SE dipped viciously, then downwards he spun at a terrific rate.

'I watched him for a short while, sickness overcoming me. It is a terrible thing to see a pal going to his death . . . Cairns was a great gentleman, and we are all very cut up. As I write this, just before packing to go home, there are tears in my eyes. Somehow, I feel I ought not to go. I ought to remain and help my flight to avenge the death of our leader – a gallant gentleman. I cannot imagine why we have no parachutes . . .'

For the RAF, June 1918 was marked by two historic events. The first was the introduction, on 3 June, of new decorations: the Distinguished Flying Cross and Air Force Cross for officers, and the Distinguished Flying Medal and Air Force Medal for other ranks. The first thirty-one DFCs had been awarded before the end of the month, as had the first DFM – awarded to Airman 1st Class (later Sergeant) W. J. Middleton, a gunner on a No 205 Squadron DH4.

The second event was the formation, on 6 June, of the Independent Force RAF, commanded by Major-General Sir Hugh Trenchard. It was the first aerial force in the world to be formed for the purpose of conducting a strategic war against the enemy without reference to or subordination by either the Army or Navy, and was the forerunner of RAF Bomber Command. The Independent Force comprised the squadrons of the former VIII Brigade, from which it was formed. Some new units had been added to its strength in May; these were Nos 99 and 104 Squadrons, both fresh out from England and equipped with DH9s.

Derived from the DH4, the DH9 had first entered service with No 103 Squadron at Old Sarum, Wiltshire, in December 1917, and had first gone into action with No 6 Squadron in France the following March. Crews soon discovered that the DH9 had a disappointing performance, mainly because its BHP engine and derivatives yielded only 230 hp instead of the anticipated 300. With a full bomb load the DH9 could barely climb to 15,000 feet, which was 7,000 feet lower than the ceiling of the DH4, which it was supposed to replace. In addition, fuel consumption above 10,000 feet was appallingly high at fifteen gallons per hour, and engine failures were rife; of twelve DH9s which set out to bomb the railway triangle at Metz-Sablon on 29 May, for example, six had been forced to turn back with engine trouble.

Although the Independent Force had a strategic task, sixty-three per cent of its sorties in June 1918 were flown against tactical targets such as rail complexes and airfields, the remaining twenty-seven per cent being flown against either the German chemical industry or the iron and steel industry. In all, seventy-seven raids were carried out during the month.

The French, too, had formed their own strategic bombing force in May, although this remained subordinate to the Army, and like the Independent Force RAF much of its effort was devoted to attacks on tactical objectives. In January, the French day bomber force, which was equipped with the excellent Breguet 14, had undergone a complete transformation, being organized into two fighting groups, each with the same structure. The first, known as the *Groupement Ménard*, comprised *Escadre de Combat* 1 and *Escadre de Bombardement* 2; the former consisted of GC 15, 18 and 19, each with four *Escadrilles* of eighteen fighters (SPAD VII or XIII), while the latter had three bomber groups, GB 5, 6 and 9, each with three *Escadrilles* of Breguets.

The other fighting group, the *Groupement Féquant*, comprised *Escadre de Combat* 2 with GC 11, 13 and 17, and *Escadre de Bombardement* 13 with two bomber groups, GB 3 and 4. By May 1918, both fighting groups had a collective total of fifty Breguet 14 day bombers and 130 fighters, the latter having the task of escorting the bombers to and from their objectives.

In that month, both fighting groups were united under the newly-created 1st Air Division, commanded by General Duval. Night bombing was undertaken by GB 1 and 2, also equipped with Breguets, and these units undertook a number of operations against industrial objectives in the Saar during the early months of 1918. The day bomber units, on the other hand, acted mainly in the support role, carrying out missions to a maximum depth of about twenty miles into enemy territory.

With the formation of the 1st Air Division, the French began to experiment with very large attack formations, two *Groupes de Chasse* usually being assigned to escort one *Escadre de Bombardement*. Difficulties at once arose: the SPAD fighters were poorly adapted to close escort work, which restricted their traditional freedom of action, and there were problems in making rendezvous with bombers at the appointed time. Another tactic employed involved the fighters sweeping ahead of the bombers to attract enemy fighters on to themselves; having disposed of the opposition, the French fighters would then make rendezvous with the bombers and escort them away from the target after they had bombed. The disadvantage here was that the bombers were left unescorted during the most dangerous part of their mission.

With these snags in mind, the French tended to adopt the close escort technique whenever possible, this being judged the lesser of two evils. The result was a large, unmanageable formation. On 16 May, for example, twenty-three Breguets of GB 9 set out on a raid preceded by thirty-six SPADs of GC 18 and followed by twenty-three more of GC 11. The whole armada trailed across five miles of sky, and when it was subjected to determined attacks by small numbers of German fighters the French aircraft simply got in each others' way and got the worst of the encounter. Years later, the Germans were to have the same experience when their fighters were tied to close escort in the Battle of Britain. The RAF adopted different and much more successful tactics when day bomber escorts were called for; the latter were usually carried out at squadron strength, or even less, and the British fighters would fly several thousand feet higher than the bombers in the hope of bouncing the enemy once they committed themselves. These tactics usually worked; but the French refused to learn, and persisted with close escort to the bitter end.

The renewal of trench warfare that followed the German spring offensive of 1918 made heavy demands on the observation squadrons of both sides, for there were entirely new trench systems to be registered and artillery emplacements to be accounted for. The RE8s of No 3 Squadron, Australian Flying Corps, were particularly effective during this period, although they suffered heavily in the process.

Sometimes they got their own back. The German artillery was beginning to entrench in the woods along the Somme between Sailly Laurette and Etinahem; counter-battery fire from the British artillery, directed by No 3 Squadron, silenced eight on 6 June and a further nine the following day. Three days later, during another counter-battery sortie, Lieutenants

Armstrong and Mart were returning to base when they noticed anti-aircraft fire near Querrieu. Armstrong flew towards the shell-bursts to investigate, and sighted a lone Halberstadt at 2,000 feet, heading east. They cut across its route and, to their astonishment, found that the German crew had no inclination to fight; they made only a feeble attempt to get away, and the Australians were able to shepherd the enemy aircraft without difficulty to Flesselles, where it made a good landing. It was something of a coup, for documents found on the captured Germans, including detailed maps, gave the order of battle of the German forces deployed against the French on the Noyon front.

On 27 June, No 3 Squadron carried out extensive photo-coverage of the Hamel area. They also pioneered a technique which was to prove of enormous value in future operations: the dropping by parachute of small-arms ammunition to Allied troops in newly-captured positions, saving the infantry a lot of effort and risk. Using information gleaned from a captured enemy document, the bomb racks of the RE8s were fitted with clips to hold two boxes each containing 2,000 rounds of .303 ammunition, above which were metal canisters for the packed parachutes. The latter were made of aeroplane fabric, with a fourteen-foot diameter and a one-foot hold at the top. The observer released the boxes via a Bowden cable and their weight pulled the parachutes from the canisters.

Trial drops were made in June by No 3 Squadron's Captain Wackett, and were so successful that the technique was quickly adopted by the remainder of the RAF's Army co-operation squadrons. On 4 July, No 9 Squadron RAF, operating from Flesselles, was detailed to drop ammunition to forward troops of the 4th Australian Division east of Nieppe. As the advance developed the troops marked the main dropping points with a white 'N', while individual machine-gun posts requiring ammunition displayed the letter 'V'.

The operation was carried out in close co-operation with No 3 Squadron. Just before dawn on the 4th, the whole squadron flew low over Hamel, dropping bombs and generally making as much noise as possible to cover the sounds of the advancing Australian Corps. The attack was over in a short time, with remarkably light casualties, and in mid-morning No 9 Squadron began its supply-dropping activities, Major J. R. Rodwell's twelve RE8s averaging four thirty-minute sorties to drop ninety-three boxes totalling 111,600 rounds on six aiming points. Refuelling and reloading – the latter carried out by a specially trained team of sixteen men – had averaged twenty minutes. Eight of the REs had supplied the main positions, while the other four had assisted the machine-gunners. The average dropping height had been 200 feet.

And, inevitably, there had been a cost. Two of the low-flying REs, braving intense enemy machine-gun fire to deliver their loads, had been shot down and their crews killed. They had begun a tradition which was to reach its highest and most tragic point of valour over a quarter of a century later, at Arnhem.

CHAPTER SEVEN

The dawn of 26 July 1918 was overcast and rainy. It did not seem as though there would be much air activity, either in the air or on the ground, so it was with some interest that a company of Welsh troops, manning the forward trenches opposite Merville, saw an aircraft flying low towards them at about six o'clock in the morning. It was an SE5, and it was immediately apparent that it was in trouble. Smoke trailed from it, and as they watched its engine stopped. It glided straight ahead and came down with a crunch in no-man's land, cartwheeling as it hit the ground.

The pilot clambered from the wreck and took refuge in a crater. Some soldiers went out to rescue him, and guided him back on all fours to the trenches. The pilot, a young New Zealander, collapsed against a trench wall, his body racked with sobs.

'The bastards have killed my Major,' he mumbled through his tears.

The unbelievable had happened; Mick Mannock was dead.

He had come back from leave to command No 85 Squadron in the first week of the month, and celebrated his return by shooting down a two-seater on the 8th. It was during this week that the Fokker D.VII first made its appearance in numbers over the front, and also the week that saw the final change of command in *Jagdgeschwader* 1; Wilhelm Reinhard was accidentally killed in a D.VII on 3 July, having scored twenty victories, and Hermann Goering took his place. It would be his bitter lot to preside over the gradual dissolution of Richthofen's fighting unit, and to witness the deaths in action, one by one, of the best German aces.

The first day of the month had seen some hectic air fighting; the weather was fine, with good visibility, and both sides were airborne in strength. One of the day's more notable air combats involved Captain J. Gilmour of No 65 Squadron, who encountered a Fokker Triplane while leading his patrol and dived on it, shooting it down in flames. Shortly afterwards he led his patrol to attack forty enemy aircraft and engaged an Albatros at point-blank range. Its wings fell off as it went into a steep dive and he turned on another, seeing it go into an upside-down spiral, apparently out of control. By this time his own aircraft had become scattered and so Gilmour decided to return to base at Bertangles. As he flew back towards the lines he was attacked by four Albatros Scouts; as the leader closed to within firing range Gilmour neatly reversed the situation by pulling up into an Immelmann turn (a stall turn followed by a half-roll, pioneered by the German ace Max Immelmann in 1915) which placed him on the enemy's tail. Gilmour fired his remaining ammunition into the Albatros, which went down to crash, and then dived for sanctuary.

There was no longer any doubt that the German pilots were, generally, of lower calibre than the men who had wrought such havoc with the Allied air arms during 1917. The mistakes they made showed it. On 1 July, for example, Captain E. J. McLaughry of No 4 Squadron AFC thought he was in for a hard time when he was attacked by three Pfalz Scouts, only to see two of them collide as they dived on him. He immediately attacked the third, which broke off the engagement and dived eastwards, and then looked for the two who had collided. He saw that one of them had crashed while the other was descending in a slow spiral, apparently still under control, if only partially so. Feeling in no mood to be merciful, the Australian fired 100 rounds into it and sent it down in flames.

Panic among the German pilots was also evident on the following day, when a patrol of five SE5s of No 60 Squadron, led by Lieutenant A. W. Saunders, sighted a formation of six Pfalz Scouts some 7,000 feet below, flying over Villers Bretonneux. Saunders led the patrol down and attacked the left-hand Pfalz, which went down and crashed after he had fired a drum of Lewis and a long burst of Vickers into it. As soon as he started his attack, the next Pfalz in line suddenly broke hard to the right and collided with the German leader. Both aircraft, tangled together, went down and crashed in the Bois de Pierret.

By early July, the fighting on the Western Front had devolved into something akin to a game of chess. After the French victory on the Aisne in June, which had come as a staggering blow to Ludendorff, the latter waited for Marshal Foch, the Allied C-in-C, to reveal his strength in some other sector, confident that he had preserved sufficient reserves to stand firm in his own battle positions. There were several weak spots in the German defences at which Foch might have struck but he was in no hurry; he could now afford to wait until there were sufficient American forces in the west to balance the total number of available German forces before launching a major offensive. In the meantime, it was for Ludendorff to make the first move.

The US 1st Division had already gone into action in May, capturing the German salient at Cantigny, north-west of Mont-didier, on the 28th. Two days later the 3rd Division had moved into the line in the Chateau-Thierry sector, followed by the 2nd Division on 2 June. On 10 June the 2nd Division carried part of Belleau Wood, south-west of Chateau-Thierry, and this initial success was completed in the last week of the month by the US Marine Brigade. There was a further American success on 1 July, when the 2nd Division captured Vaux, at the corner of the Marne salient, and took 450 prisoners. On the 4th, American troops were brigaded with British forces for the first time, and General Monash's Australian Corps, together with US troops of General Bell's 33rd Division, captured Hamel and took over 1,500 prisoners between them. Also on 4 July, an appropriate date in American history, the arrival of more US forces in the line permitted the US First Army Corps to be regrouped; it now comprised the 1st, 2nd, 3rd, 4th, 26th and 28th Divisions.

There had been changes in the American air commitment in France, too. Since 24 May, the US air arm had no longer been part of the Signal Corps; it was now the US Army Air Service, and was commanded by Major General William Kenley, himself a pilot. By July 1918 the American First Pursuit Group in France had been expanded to five squadrons, the 27th, 94th, 95th, 147th and 185th, the latter reserved for night fighting. They were initially equipped with Nieuport 28s, but later exchanged these for SPADs, which could meet the Fokker

D.VII on much more favourable terms. The American Expeditionary Force's First Observation Group, formed in the summer of 1918, used the Salmson 2A reconnaissance biplane, and eleven squadrons were eventually equipped with it; the US day bomber squadrons, like their French counterparts, used the Breguet 14.

When Ludendorff's expected attack came, it fell upon the French and Americans, and consequently it was their squadrons which bore the brunt of the air fighting in mid-July. The last great German offensive of the war began on 15 July on a fifty-mile front to the east and west of Reims, the main German thrust aiming to cross the Marne. The attack was preceded by a bombardment of furious intensity, its thunder awakening the inhabitants of Paris in the early hours of the morning.

The Allied air units were rapidly concentrated to meet the threat. The *Cigognes* were quickly transferred to a forward airstrip, Trécon in the Chateau-Thierry sector, while nine RAF squadrons flew southwards through rainstorms a few hours before the opening of the battle proper. Much of the RAF's effort was devoted to airfield attacks; during the morning, for example, Nos 65 and 209 Squadrons, escorted by Nos 23, 24 and 84 Squadrons, dropped 105 25-lb bombs on Foucaucourt aerodrome and fired 8,300 rounds into hangars and other buildings in a series of low-level attacks. Many direct hits were obtained, and two hangars set on fire. All the RAF aircraft returned safely, shooting down two enemy balloons on the way back.

Despite determined attacks such as these, the German Flying Corps operated in strength throughout the offensive, and suffered substantial casualties. JG 1 'Richthofen' was in the area opposite Chateau-Thierry, and before the month was out it had lost seven of its leading pilots. Lieutenant Fritz Friedrichs of *Jasta* 10, with twenty-one victories, was shot down and killed on the day the attack started, while Lieutenant Hans Kirchstein (twenty-seven victories) and *Vizefeldwebel* (Warrant Officer) Fritz Krebs, with six victories, were lost on the following day. Both pilots belonged to *Jasta* 6.

Of all the German aces who remained in 1918, one seemed to bear a charmed life. Ernst Udet had scored his twentieth victory in April and had been awarded the coveted *Pour le*

Mérite; since then his rise had been truly meteoric. He led his *Jasta* 4 into action like a tiger, piling up victories, and in the summer he formed a deadly combination with the new Fokker D.VII and was to end the war as the top-scoring German pilot after von Richthofen, with sixty-two kills. After the war he went on to achieve international fame as a test, sporting and aerobatic pilot. In 1935 he joined the new *Luftwaffe* and was eventually appointed to the post of Director-General of Equipment. The fact that he had little talent for organization became plain in the early months of the Russian campaign in 1941, when his department failed to produce aircraft to make good the heavy German losses. In continual conflict with both Hitler and Hermann Goering, his former commanding officer in JG 1, he became increasingly depressed and committed suicide on 17 November, 1941 – a sad end for a man who, at the close of a brilliant flying career, had become a square peg in a round hole.

Another German ace who rose to the highest command in Hitler's *Luftwaffe* was Robert, Ritter von Greim, who commanded *Jasta* 34, JG 10, and ended the war with twenty-eight victories. In April 1945, with the *Luftwaffe* tottering to its collapse, he was appointed by Hitler to succeed Goering as its C-in-C. Taken prisoner by the Allies, he committed suicide in June.

One man who was to play a prominent part in shaping the *Luftwaffe* in the years between the wars was Wolfram von Richthofen on *Jasta* 11, the cousin of Manfred. He ended the war with eight victories and, in 1936, commanded the Kondor Legion in Spain. This was followed by an appointment as C-in-C *Fliegerkorps* VIII, in which he brought dive-bombing operations with the Junkers Ju 87 *Stuka* to a fine art during the Polish and French campaigns. He successively commanded *Luftflotte* 4 and *Luftflotte* 2, the latter in the Mediterranean Theatre, but he contracted a brain tumour and died in July 1945 after being transferred to the reserve at the end of the previous year.

The air battles of July 1918 established René Fonck for all time as France's ace of aces. On the 16th, as he was flying to join the *Cigognes* at Trécon – he had just been recalled from leave in Paris – he sighted a pair of LVG two-seaters directly over the lines, with six Fokker D.VIIs 1,500 feet higher up. Despite the fact that his SPAD was encumbered by two suitcases and a case of wine, stuffed under his feet in the cockpit, he decided to attack. Ignoring the Fokkers, he made one pass against the two-seaters and sent both of them down in flames. The Fokkers pursued him, bent on revenge, but he outran them and made a safe landing at Trécon, his precious bottles intact. During the next three days, Fonck destroyed a further five enemy aircraft, bringing his score so far to fifty-six.

Charles Nungesser was now trailing a long way behind Fonck. He scored his fortieth victory on 16 July, but no more Germans would fall to him that month. He was physically worn out, and a day later the doctors sent him away for a rest. Like so many other pilots in this war, Nungesser suffered from bouts of continual sickness; much of it was brought on by nervous strain, but the real culprit was the castor oil used to lubricate the early aero-engines, which was spewed out and inhaled by pilots in considerable quantities. It had a terribly debilitating effect, and many who survived the war continued to suffer from it in later life.

Close behind Nungesser came Georges Madon, who destroyed his thirty-seventh aircraft on 17 July. He might have been justified in claiming three more, because he was instrumental in their destruction, although he never fired a shot at them. Shortly before he claimed his confirmed victim, a two-seater, he sighted three Pfalz Scouts flying in formation near Epernay and dived out of the sun to attack them. Two broke violently in opposite directions and collided head-on, their tangled remains drifting down to crash. The third tried to escape by means of a high-speed dive, a fatal thing to do in a Pfalz. The resulting structural failure was catastrophic and the aircraft fell apart, its fragments falling over a wide area.

The next day, Madon destroyed a Fokker D.VII over Main-de-Massignes, a location on the Champagne downs. Its pilot was Lieutenant Moritz Bretschneider-Bodener, a member of JG 1's *Jasta* 6, who had five aircraft to his credit.

At first, the German offensive had all the hallmarks of success. The initial advance was rapid; the Germans overwhelmed the first line of defence and then, seeing that most of the French positions were deserted and that resistance ahead was solid, began to realize that they were being sucked into a trap. On 18 July Marshal Foch launched his counter-stroke on a twenty-seven mile front between Fontenoy and Belleau, west of Chateau-Thierry. General Mangin's French Tenth Army, which included the 1st and 2nd US Infantry Divisions, penetrated eight miles into the enemy front, taking 5,000 prisoners, while south of this the Franco-American forces under General Degoutte made an advance of three to five miles. Both moves were heavily supported by tanks, 324 of which were engaged in the Tenth Army's sector.

On 19 July a strong British reserve force arrived to take part in the battle near Reims, going into the line in a sector which had been gallantly defended by Italian troops; the latter had completely destroyed a German division and severely mauled several others. The British force struck along the Ardre river valley at Marfaux, which they won, lost and partly recaptured, and also took Courfon Wood. Strong German forces from the Champagne sector checked the British left, but the centre and right fought onward, taking St Euphraise village and Bouilly across the Reims road and threatening the main German communications route running from Fismes and the Ardre valley to the Marne front.

The unexpected British pressure forced the Germans into a rapid retreat across the Marne for the second time in the war. The timely intervention of the British completely brought to an end the vast scheme of operations started by Ludendorff in March and changed the whole face of the war by throwing the Germans on the defensive. By a fitting coincidence, it was one of the British formations that had helped to stem the first German assault in March – the Scottish Highland Territorial Division – that now took part in the counter-stroke that threw the enemy into disarray.

As the Germans retreated over the Marne the Franco-American forces closed round Chateau-Thierry, entering the battered town on 21 July. In the next two days they advanced towards Fere and Oulchy by a southern flanking movement through La Croix, Rocourt and Epieds, cutting the Soissons road in a swaying battle of thrust and counter-thrust that ended, on 28 July, in a magnificent action by the 17th French Division and the 15th Scottish Division, attached to General Mangin's army, who between them stormed and took Grand Rozoy ridge, a critical point in the enemy's defensive line.

Throughout this period of incessant fighting, the Allied air arms maintained pressure on the enemy's airfields, on both the Marne and the Somme. In one spectacular operation on 22 July, Major Raymond Collishaw and Captain L. H. Rochford of No 203 Squadron set out at 3.40 am to attack the aerodrome at Dorignies. Rochford attacked first, firing all his ammunition into the buildings and hangars from 200 feet, and then dropped three Cooper bombs on some barracks and a fourth on a hangar, which went on fire. Collishaw, beginning his run, spotted three aircraft that were being pulled from a hangar and machine-gunned them, after which he dropped four bombs from 150 feet among the barrack huts. Turning, he saw an enemy aircraft approaching to land and attacked it, shooting it down in flames. Two hours later, he returned to survey the damage; three Albatros Scouts were patrolling the airfield and attacked him, but he shot one down in flames and made his escape. Later in the day, Captain Rochford also destroyed a Fokker D.VII, and four more – the remainder of the enemy formation – were either shot down or driven down out of control by the other pilots of his patrol, Lieutenants W. Sidebottom and A. E. Rudge.

This period saw the arrival on the Western Front of two RAF fighter squadrons which were to make their mark in the annals of the Service. No 92 Squadron, equipped with SE5s, arrived at Drionville, south-west of St Omer, on 19 July, and three days later its first kill – a Fokker D.VII – was scored by one of its flight commanders, Captain J. M. Robb (later Air Marshal Sir James Robb).

The second squadron was the RAF's first specialist night-fighter unit. No 151 Squadron was formed at Hainault Farm on 12 June 1918 by combining one flight each from Nos 44, 78 and 112 Squadrons, its purpose being to counter enemy night attacks on British bases on the Western Front. Its first success was scored by Captain A. B. Yuille, flying a Sopwith Camel, who sighted and attacked a Gotha in the early hours of 25 July. The Gotha crash-landed behind the British lines with both engines out of action and its observer wounded. In the months that followed, No 151 Squadron was to carry out many night interceptions, as well as mounting night intruder operations against the German bomber airfields, and by the end of the war its pilots had claimed the destruction of twenty-six enemy aircraft. It was to remain a night-fighter unit for most of its career, and the last aircraft it used in this role in the late 1950s was the potent Gloster Javelin all-weather jet fighter – a far cry from the Camels with which it pioneered its night-fighting techniques.

By the time No 151 Squadron arrived in France, German heavier-than-air bombing raids on Britain had ended. The last one had occurred on the night of 20/21 May, when twenty-eight Gothas and three Giants set out to attack London. They were met by a vastly more effective night-fighter force than had been the case three or four months earlier, at the time of the previous night raids: seventy-four Camels and SE5s in place of the mediocre BE2cs which had opposed the bombers earlier. The fighters shot down three Gothas, the anti-aircraft guns two, and a sixth crashed in Essex after engine failure. It was the biggest loss suffered by the German bombers in a single night's operations over England, and it was to be more than two decades before they came again.

On 25 July, Taffy Jones of No 74 Squadron flew over to visit his former CO, Mick Mannock, at No 85 Squadron's base. 'I can't quite make out whether he has got nerves or not,' he wrote later. 'One minute, he's full-out. The next, he gives the impression of being morbid, and keeps bringing up his pet subject of being shot down in flames. I told him I had got a two-seater in flames on patrol this morning before breakfast. "Could you hear the sod scream?" he asked with a sour smile. "One day, they'll get you like that, my lad. You are getting careless. Don't forget to blow your brains out." Everyone roared with laughter . . .'

At 5.30 the next morning, Mick Mannock, patrolling at 5,000 feet over Merville with Lieutenant D. C. Inglis, a young New Zealander from Canterbury who had yet to shoot down his first German, sighted a Junkers CL.1 two-seater, an angular, all-metal low-wing monoplane which was just beginning to enter service with the German ground-attack squadrons. Mannock, after pointing it out to Inglis, led the New Zealander down to attack, diving and then climbing up under

104

the Junkers' tail. The German aircraft soon caught fire and spun down to crash.

Mannock, contrary to his usual practice, followed it down, firing at it as it fell. He and Inglis strafed the wreck as it lay burning on the ground, then flew at low level – no more than 200 feet – towards no-man's land, zig-zagging as they went to avoid the intense small-arms fire that was being directed at them from the enemy positions.

Suddenly, near Colonne, Inglis saw the nose of Mannock's SE5 go down. The left wing dropped slowly, and now Inglis could see a small flicker of flame and a ribbon of smoke coming from the aircraft's starboard side. The SE5 went into a spin and crashed among some trenches, bursting into flames on impact. Distraught, Inglis circled the wreckage several times, but there was no hope that Mannock might have survived. The New Zealander turned for home, crash-landing in no-man's land after being hit by ground fire.

On the day that Mannock died, the Germans lost another of their leading aces, but *Vizefeldwebel* Kurt Wusthoff of *Jasta* 4 – a pilot with twenty-seven victories – was more fortunate. He was shot down by René Fonck, but survived to become a prisoner of war. Fonck paid him a visit in hospital, where the German admitted to him that although the Frenchman's fame had spread throughout the German Flying Corps, no one had any idea of the tactics he used.

'That's hardly surprising,' Fonck told him wryly. 'When I attack someone, he doesn't usually live to talk about it.'

By the end of July 1918, the Allies had succeeded in turning defeat into victory, or at least the beginning of victory. Soon, the long misery of trench warfare would be over; the battle now would be for village after village, town after town, as the Germans were pushed steadily back across the ground they had gained. August would be a crucial month, and one that would witness, in the air, the heaviest losses suffered by both sides since the great spring battles of 1917.

CHAPTER EIGHT

The battle for Amiens was in full swing, and the RAF's observation crews were working as hard, if not harder, than they had ever done. Losses were high, and many crews were lucky to escape with their lives as they operated at low level in search of the enemy. One such crew consisted of Captain Ferdinand West – known to everyone as Freddie – and his observer, Lieutenant John Haslam; on 8 and 9 August they made two reconnaissance flights in their Armstrong Whitworth F.K.8 of No 8 Squadron, Vignacourt, and each time their aircraft was so badly damaged by ground fire that they had to crash-land, escaping with no more than shock and a few bruises.

The next day they were sent out again on another reconnaissance, keeping an eye open for the enemy fighters that were reported to be very active over the battlefront. Freddie West was not complacent about them, but neither did he fear them unduly; the 'Big Ack' was a tough nut to crack, and he had developed his own tactics to counter the enemy's, as he explained:

'They invariably followed the same tactics. Once they spotted you they went up to about five or six hundred feet above you and then they tried to dive on you, all guns blazing, and shoot you down. Our way to answer was that the observer should open fire immediately he saw the German pilot put his nose down. Often the pilots didn't like being fired at; they broke combat. Occasionally, you had a tougher fellow who wanted to go on fighting. In that case I would try to do a very unpleasant flat turn and try to face the direction the enemy was coming from, because that compelled him to do large turns to the left or to the right and give my observer a chance to fire on him. That's the way we tried to save ourselves.'

On this particular August day, the task of West and Haslam was to locate the enemy's reserves near Amiens, a job that involved flying at 1,500 feet over enemy territory. West described what happened subsequently.

'I was lucky, or unlucky, whichever way you want to look at it, and I was delighted to find at last an area where I saw many German troops, a large amount of transport, a large amount of guns – and I thought, this is the information that the army needs. And so, having got this information, I made straight for my aerodrome. Unfortunately, German fighters were also of the opinion that I should not bring back this information and so I was attacked. During one fight I received some explosive bullets in my left leg, which was almost severed, but you know when you are young you are an optimist, and I think the combination of youth, health and optimism got me back. I am also grateful to my observer who did first-class work with his Lewis guns and I'm glad to have this opportunity to pay a tribute to him, because he is still alive. We may be, for all I know, the only alive team from the 1914–18 war in the air. He became a group captain and a parson. He's a reverend, probably due to my bad language in the aeroplane.'

What West, with typical modesty, does not say in this account is that he was attacked by seven enemy aircraft, and that despite being wounded in the foot, and his aircraft damaged, he made another circuit of the area to make sure of the enemy dispositions. On the way back to base he came under continual attack, and his virtually severed left leg fell among the controls. He lifted it clear and twisted his clothing into a tourniquet with one hand, flying the aircraft with the other, and managed to land on a patch of grass close to some Canadian positions. Desperately weak from loss of blood, he insisted on making his report before being taken to hospital, where his leg was amputated. Haslam was also wounded in the ankle, but not seriously.

Freddie West was later awarded the Victoria Cross. After the war, fitted with an artificial leg, he resigned himself to a legal career, but with the help of Sir Hugh Trenchard he came back into the RAF and regained his flying category. He served as air attaché in Finland, Estonia and Latvia, and on the outbreak of the 1939–45 War he was a station commander in No 2 Group, RAF Bomber Command, with the rank of group captain. He subsequently served on clandestine duties in Switzerland, where he was involved with the RAF's 'escape line', and eventually retired as an air commodore.

The allied offensive that began on 8 August 1918 was later described by Ludendorff, in his memoirs, as the 'black day of the German Army'. On that day, General Rawlinson's 4th British Army and the 1st French Army under General Débeney attacked on a fifteen-mile front east of Amiens. By three o'clock in the afternoon the Allied forces had made advances of up to seven miles and taken 7,000 prisoners; the offensive was supported by 430 tanks, the whole of the British Tank Corps less one brigade.

During the week preceding the offensive, the Allied air forces made numerous attacks on enemy airfields, particularly those occupied by the *Schlachtstaffeln*. In the early hours of 1 August, two Camels of No 151 Squadron, flown by Captain S. Cockerell and Captain W. H. Haynes, carried out intruder patrols over Estrées and Guizancourt aerodromes; Cockerell arrived over Estrées just as an enemy aircraft was landing and dropped a bomb, which burst about fifty yards away from it, and then came back round and fired 200 rounds at it from close range. At that moment all the lights went out and Cockerell was unable to see any result, so he dropped two more bombs in the hope of hitting something before returning to base. Shortly afterwards Haynes also appeared over Estrées, having found nothing worthwhile at the other airfield, and attacked one of three Gothas which he saw approaching. The Gotha sheered off and he lost it. He dropped his bombs on a searchlight battery and then also headed for home, his guns having jammed.

A much more successful airfield attack was carried out at dawn, when the Camels of Nos 3 and 56 Squadrons, escorted by No 11 Squadron (Bristol Fighters) and No 60 Squadron (SE5s) dropped 104 25-lb bombs on Epinoy. All four squadrons then strafed the airfield, firing hundreds of rounds into the hangars, billets, workshops and the officers' mess. Two hangars received direct hits from bombs and six more were set on fire in the strafing attacks, the pilots claiming the destruction of seventeen enemy aircraft on the ground. Two very large fires were started in the workshops, and photo reconnaissance later showed a pall of smoke rising to 10,000 feet over the enemy base. It is interesting to note that Nos 3 and 56 Squadrons, both of which were based at Valheureux, made a very effective partnership in this kind of operation; over a quarter of a century later, the same two units, flying Hawker Tempests as part of the 2nd Tactical Air Force's No 122 Wing, were also to wreak havoc with enemy airfields on the continent in the dying months of World War Two.

The next night, two Camels of No 151 Squadron again visited Estrées and Guizancourt. The first to arrive was Major C. J. Q. Brand, who dropped two bombs on the hangars at Guizancourt and then attacked a large two-seater which was coming in to land. He attacked it again on the ground, but broke off when all the lights went out. He remained in the vicinity of the airfield for the next half hour, dropping two bombs in the path of an aircraft which was about to touch down, then strafed the hangars and searchlights. Shortly afterwards he attacked another enemy aircraft, but was himself attacked from the rear by a German scout and returned to base. In the 1939–45 War, this officer – then Air Vice-Marshal Sir Quinton Brand DSO, MC, DFC – was to command No 10 Group, RAF Fighter Command, in the Battle of Britain.

The other Camel of No 151 Squadron that night was flown by Captain Cockerell, who dropped four bombs on the hangars at Guizancourt and then shot up four searchlights until they went out. Soon afterwards he attacked a Gotha, which crash-landed some distance from the airfield.

The week from 5th to 11th August saw the heaviest losses on both sides, the RAF alone claiming the destruction of 177 enemy aircraft, with a further 90 driven down out of control, for the loss of 150 of their own. Almost every RAF bomber formation that set out was heavily attacked by enemy fighters, and as the Germans retired to new positions intense ground fire took its toll of the observation squadrons. The new Fokker D.VIIs were very much in evidence; on 8 August nine of them attacked an RE8 of No 3 Squadron AFC and shot it down, killing its crew, and on the following day the DH9s of No 49 Squadron were subjected to persistent attacks by two large formations of Fokkers as they returned from a bombing raid. One crew – Lieutenant J. A. Keating (an American officer) and 2nd Lieutenant E. A. Simpson had a particularly hard time, and it was only the observer's skill that saved them. Simpson shot down a Fokker in flames at close range, followed by another shortly afterwards, and during the running fight that followed he sent two more down to crash. By this time the DH9 had been practically shot to ribbons, and he was lucky to make a forced landing on the right side of the lines.

On the opening day of the offensive, many RAF units were assigned to ground-attack work. Among them was No 43 Squadron, its Camels now carrying an increased bomb load of four 25-lb bombs. One of its pilots, Lieutenant Ben Lefroy, had a very lucky escape:

'I had done my work for the day, two sorties, and was reading my mail in the mess. An orderly came haring in and asked for volunteers as a pilot in A Flight had gone sick. As the only person in the mess – it was me! The only machine I could get was "R", the target practice machine, a slow and bad machine. My own Camel was being repaired, having collected some Hun bullets on my previous sortie. Soon after coming out of cloud we ran into fifteen Huns. My engine was not good, and trying to get more out of it I "choked" it. At this time I saw Cecil King with a couple of Huns on his tail and so pulled up to give 'em a squirt and down they came on me. The universal joint was shot off the joystick, my rudder wires cut, and petrol was squirting all over the cockpit. With the throttle I kept pulling the nose up until, at 300 feet, I went into a spin and went in. I came to four hours later, in our barrage, with a Hun by my side. I had three bullet holes in me, both knees out of joint, fractured skull and fractured wrist – and of course a P.O.W.'

On 12 August, No 43 Squadron at Fienvillers became the first RAF unit in France to receive a fighter that was at last capable of meeting the German Flying Corps' Fokker D.VIIs and Siemens-Schuckert D.IIIs on more than equal terms – the Sopwith Snipe. Conceived in 1917 as a replacement for the Camel, six prototypes of the Snipe had been ordered in the autumn of that year, but a number of modifications had proven necessary and it wa is not until the spring of 1918 that the Snipe entered production. With 230 hp available from its very reliable Bentley BR2 rotary engine the Snipe was a potent weapon for its day, although like the Camel it was by no means easier to handle. Standard armament comprised two synchronized Vickers guns mounted in front of the cockpit. With a top speed of over 120 mph, an operational ceiling of over 19,500 feet and an endurance of three hours, its performance over the Camel was greatly improved – as was the visibility from the cockpit, a vital asset from the pilot's point of view. No 43 Squadron was eventually to receive twenty-four aircraft, but it would be the middle of September before the last one was delivered and so, as the new aircraft were initially permitted to fly only defensive patrols on the British side of the lines, the Camels remained in service for some time longer.

On 8 August, the first day of the British offensive, the RAF lost forty-five aircraft in combat, with a further fifty-two wrecked on landing, a wastage rate of more than thirteen per cent. Casualties among the low-flying squadrons were particularly high, reaching twenty-three per cent. Many of the losses were sustained in attacks on the bridges over the Somme, across which the Germans were retreating in considerable confusion; the tragedy was that not one of the bridges was hit. It was not until the afternoon of 9 August that a hit was at last registered on the bridge at Brie, by a DH4 of No 205 Squadron.

There were some extraordinary adventures during those first two days of the battle. One pilot of No 24 Squadron, for example, was forced down after bombing some German infantry with a hole in his SE5's main fuel tank. He managed to fend off the Germans with his revolver until he switched to the auxiliary tank, which held enough fuel to take him to the British lines. Other pilots, like one officer of No 209 Squadron, abandoned their damaged aircraft and fought on foot alongside British troops – although one, Lieutenant McKay of No 201 Squadron, wisely decided that discretion was the better part of valour. Shot down by four Fokker D.VIIs three hundred yards behind the enemy lines, he saw an advancing British tank and made a dash for it. When he learned that it was about to go into action, he jumped off again and zig-zagged through streams of heavy machine-gun fire to reach the British lines, out of breath but otherwise unharmed.

On 11 August, Lieutenant C. V. Gardner of No 19 Squadron attacked one of four Pfalz Scouts, which burst into flames.

111

Gardner saw the German pilot jump from the cockpit and deploy a parachute, the first time this had been seen in an escape from an aircraft. It is not known whether the enemy pilot landed safely. The first recorded instance of a pilot escaping by parachute from an aircraft, and surviving, occurred on 22 August, when Lieutenant Frigyes Hefty of the 42nd Fighter Squadron, Austro-Hungarian Air Corps, jumped from his burning Albatros D.III after a fight with Italian Hanriots over the Piave River; he made a heavy landing, but suffered no serious injury.

The German Flying Corps suffered appalling losses during these crucial days of August 1918. Among the pilots killed was Erich Loewenhardt, commanding *Jasta* 10 of JG 1; by the beginning of August 1918 he had scored fifty-three victories, making him the third-ranking German ace after Richthofen and Udet. He was shot down on the morning of 10 August by Captain Henry Burden of No 56 Squadron during a fight between the unit's SE5s and JG 1's D.VIIs. Burden shot down two more enemy aircraft that morning, and two more later in the day. RAF pilots reported that the elite German fighter units seemed to have thrown caution to the winds in their efforts to establish air superiority over the battlefront; this was later confirmed by the biographer of Hermann Goering, who later wrote that 'With a real contempt for death, the Squadron suffered terrible losses owing to its reckless behaviour.'

By 11 August the Allied offensive petered out as German resistance stiffened, but it had already cost the enemy 22,000 prisoners and 400 guns. The battle itself had not been decisive, but it had hammered the first nail in the coffin of enemy morale. The German soldiers, at all levels, knew that from now on there could be no question that Germany might win the war. All she might hope to achieve now was some kind of stalemate.

The recently-blooded United States Army Air Service combat squadrons were active during the battles of August, and their leading fighter pilots were fast emerging. Heading the list was Lieutenant Eddie Rickenbacker, who had several victories to his credit by the time the First Pursuit Group re-equipped with SPADs in August. However, one of the most creditable achievements in that month by an American pilot was on the first day, when Lieutenant Donald Hudson of the 27th Aero Squadron destroyed three enemy aircraft. His combat report tells the story:

'We were attacked by eight Fokker biplane Chasse machines east of Fère-en-Tardenois at 8.10 am. I tried to bank to the left and fell into a spin, and when I came out there were four enemy aircraft on my tail. I tried to turn again but fell into another spin. I was followed by the four EA down to 1,000 m. As I was coming out of the spin a machine was headed straight at me. I fired and he turned to the left; I turned a little to the left and turned back again being right on his tail. I fired about 20 rounds into him. He fell off slowly on his right wing and went into a spin. I turned on the other machines and went into a spin. When I came out the other machines were climbing up. Just as the fight began I saw an enemy plane fall off on his right wing and spin in exactly the same manner as the machine I shot down. I saw something else fall in flames. A SPAD passed within 20 feet of my right wing, falling on its back. My engine was boiling and I could not climb as my Nourrice (coolant) was empty and by using the hand pump I just about kept going. Then north-east of the railroad between Fère-en-Tardenois and Spaoney, I encountered a Rumpler biplane at between 100 and 200 m. He passed me on the right and banked up to give his observer a good shot at me. I turned and got on his tail and followed him in a circle firing right into his cockpit. Suddenly his right wing came off and he crashed. I was being fired at by machine-guns on the ground and was essing (weaving) when I noticed another Rumpler under me to my left. I turned down and fired at the observer. He disappeared and the machine crashed just beside the railroad embankment. I circled the machine once to see if either the pilot or the observer got out, but they did not.'

One young American who had his first taste of air combat in August was Lieutenant Frank Luke, a boy from Arizona who, in a brief seventeen-day period of action, was to destroy eighteen enemy aircraft and balloons. Yet his first combat, on 16 August, was not particularly auspicious. His report reads:

'Saw Hun formation and followed, getting above, into the sun. The formation was strung out leaving one machine way in the rear. Being way above the formation, I cut my motor and dove down on the rear

113

man, keeping the sun directly behind. Opened fire at about a hundred feet, keeping both guns on him until to within a few feet, then zoomed away. When I next saw him he was on his back, but looked as though he was going to come out of it, so I dove again, holding both guns on him. Instead of coming out of it he side-slipped off the opposite side, much like a falling leaf, and went down on his back.

'My last dive carried me out of reach of another machine that had turned about. They gave chase for about five minutes, then turned back, for I was leading them. My last look at the plane shot down convinced me that he struck the ground, for he was still on his back about 1,500 metres below.

'On coming home above our lines saw four EA. Started to get into the sun and above, but they saw me and dove towards me. I peaked for home. Three turned back and the other came on. I kept out of range by peaking slightly and he followed me to Coincy, where he saw one of the 95th (Squadron) boys and turned about. The 95th man could have brought down this EA if he had realized quick enough that it was an EA . . .'

Because the aircraft shot down by Luke had fallen in enemy territory, near Soissons, he could not claim it as a victory, and in fact came in for a certain amount of ridicule from his squadron mates when he pressed the claim. His colleagues were not impressed by Luke at all during those early days; he was too cocksure and arrogant for their liking, and his squadron commander referred to him on one occasion as 'the damndest nuisance that ever stepped on to a flying field'. It only made Luke more determined than ever to excel, and he soon proved that he was capable of doing it by making his speciality one of the most difficult and dangerous targets of all – the enemy's observation balloons.

While men like Frank Luke helped to turn the tide of the air war overwhelmingly in the Allies' favour, those who had been fighting it for a long time took the opportunity to add to their scores in August's battles. In the *Cigognes*, René Fonck remained the master of his trade, destroying his fifty-seventh aircraft on 1 August. With the start of the Allied offensive the French pilots were mostly engaged in ground-attack work and there were few air combats in their sector, although Georges Madon shot down a Fokker D.VII flown by Lieutenant Max

Festler of *Jasta* 13 on 11 August and several more enemy aircraft were destroyed by other pilots.

On 14 August, Charles Nungesser, breaking his Parisian leave against doctor's orders, suddenly arrived at the *Cigognes*' airfield with the announcement that he had no intention of missing all the fun. That same day, he shot down four German *Drachen* observation balloons, receiving a slight wound on his last sortie. But René Fonck, not to be outdone, shot down three enemy aircraft that day in the space of ten seconds; all three fell burning in a field, separated by less than a hundred yards. The pilots were later identified as Lieutenant Friedrich, Warrant Officer Arnold and Corporal Horber.

The next day, 15 August, Charles Nungesser scored his forty-fifth victory. Accompanied by Warrant Officer Henriot and Sergeant Millot, he pounced on a Fokker D.VII flown by *Vizefeldwebel* Fritz Scheide and sent it down in flames. That night, in the *Cigognes*' mess, Nungesser admitted that he was feeling ill. 'But,' he said, 'I've no intention of dying before I get my fiftieth German.'

For Nungesser, however, there would be no more victories. His body had taken too much of a battering over the past years, and he would never again fly in combat.

Airfield attacks by day continued to be attended by success, as two extracts from the official RAF summary reveal:

'*August 13th*. A raid was carried out by 17th American Squadron on Varssenaere Aerodrome, in conjunction with squadrons of the 5th Group. After the first two squadrons had dropped their bombs from a low height, machines of 17th American Squadron dived to within 200 feet of the ground and released their bombs, then proceeded to shoot at hangars and huts on the aerodrome, and a chateau on the NE corner of the aerodrome was also attacked with machine-gun fire. The following damage was observed to be caused by this combined operation: A dump of petrol and oil was set on fire, which appeared to set fire to an ammunition dump; six Fokker biplanes were set on fire on the ground, and two destroyed by direct hits from bombs; one large Gotha hangar was set on fire and another half demolished; a living hut was set on fire and several hangars were seen to be smouldering as a result of phosphorus bombs having fallen on them. In spite of most of the machines taking part being hit at one time or another, all returned safely, favourable ground targets being attacked on the way home. No 211 Squadron (DH4s) bombed the aerodrome after the low flying attack was over, and demolished the chateau previously referred to.

'*August 16th*. A raid was carried out on Haubourdin Aerodrome by Nos 88 and 92 Squadrons RAF and Nos 2 and 4 Squadrons AFC. Sixty-five machines took part in all, dropping 136 25-lb and six 40-lb bombs and firing a large number of rounds from a height varying from 400 to 50 feet. Three large hangars containing machines were completely burnt, and two machines standing outside were set on fire. Several fires were also started in huts, and what is believed to be the officers' mess was blown up and burnt. Several other hangars, in addition to those burnt, received direct hits. The station at Haubourdin was also attacked with machine-gun fire from a low height, causing confusion among the troops. Two staff cars were fired at, one of which upset in a ditch and another ran up a steep bank; the occupants were not observed to leave. A train was also shot at, which stopped. Considerable casualties were caused among the personnel at the aerodrome, who were seen rushing to take refuge in a hospital. All our machines returned.'

Night bombing in August 1918 was attended by mixed fortunes, although the Independent Force's striking power had now been boosted with the arrival in France of three more squadrons, Nos 97, 115 and 215, all equipped with the Handley Page 0/400. A development of the 0/100, the 0/400 was powered by two 360 hp Rolls-Royce Eagle engines, which gave it a maximum speed of 95 mph and an operational ceiling of 8,500 feet. Defensive armament comprised one or two Lewis guns mounted in both nose and rear cockpits; in the latter position one gun was fired sideways or backwards from a raised platform while the second could be fired downwards through a trapdoor in the fuselage floor. The 0/400 carried a maximum bomb load of 2,000 lb and was fitted with a new bomb sight designed by Lieutenant-Commander Wimperis; the Drift Sight Mk 1A took account of the aircraft's height above the target, its airspeed, wind velocity and drift. It was far from efficient, but it was a vast improvement on the rudimentary equipment used previously.

The arrival of this new equipment enabled the Independent

116

Force to step up its night bombing effort. However, the DH9s were still heavily committed to day bombing missions against strategic targets and took increasingly heavy punishment, especially since the potent Siemens-Schuckert D.III fighter had now returned to operational service after undergoing modifications and equipped *Jastas* 4a, 4b, 5, 6 and 8, all assigned to the defence of German industrial targets.

At 7.30 am on 22 August, thirteen DH9s of No 104 Squadron set out from Azelot in two formations of six and seven aircraft to bomb the BASF factory at Mannheim. One aircraft in the rear flight turned back over the lines with engine trouble, and soon afterwards another was shot down by heavy anti-aircraft fire. Then the fire died away as eight enemy scouts appeared; they remained on the flanks of the formation, waiting to pick off stragglers and contenting themselves with exchanging a few shots at long range. Their chance came when the DH9 flown by Lieutenant J. Valentine suffered engine failure; they pounced on him as he broke formation and glided down, but he survived intense attacks to make a forced landing behind the enemy lines. Over the Vosges Mountains a third DH9, piloted by Captain McKay, 'B' Flight commander, also had engine failure and had to come down, the crew being taken prisoner.

The remaining DH9s approached Mannheim at 11,500 feet. As they started their bombing run they were attacked by fifteen Fokker and Pfalz Scouts, SSW D.IIIs and Halberstadt two-seaters. In the ensuing battle the RAF formation was broken up and forced down to 6,000 feet, where two of the scattered bombers were quickly shot down. The five surviving aircraft managed to fight their way back to base, but it had been a black day for the squadron, which had lost seven out of twelve DH9s and most of its best aircrew.

Yet the DH9 could give an excellent account of itself. The next day, an aircraft of No 49 Squadron, returning from a bombing raid and crewed by Lieutenant A. R. Spurling and Sergeant F. W. Bell, became separated from the rest of the formation in cloud. After flying west for some time, Spurling saw what he took to be a friendly airfield and prepared to land, but as he lost height he was suddenly attacked by a Fokker D.VII. Spurling then saw a formation of thirty more D.VIIs directly below him and, with little other option, continued his dive through the middle of them, firing as he went. One of the Fokkers was hit and burst into flames; two more, taking violent evasive action, went into a spin and one of them was seen to crash. The DH9 was then harried from astern by four Fokkers, one of which was shot down in flames by Sergeant Bell; a few moments later Bell also accounted for another which attempted a beam attack. The DH9 was pursued by three more D.VIIs as it climbed hard towards the lines, but they did not attack. An enemy two-seater tried to intercept it as it headed for home, but a few well-aimed bursts from Bell drove it away.

There was a particularly effective night bombing attack on the night of 25/26 August, when two 0/400s of No 215 Squadron set out from Xaffervillers to attack the Badische Anilin Works at Mannheim. The plan was well co-ordinated, and called for the first aircraft, flown by Captain W. B. Lawson, to approach Mannheim at 5,000 feet and draw the enemy fire. As soon as he was joined by the second 0/400, flown by Lieutenant M. C. Purvis, Lawson was to leave the target area and shut down his engines, gliding back from a distance of four miles, which was calculated to bring him over the target at 1,000 feet. In fact, Lawson mistimed his glide and arrived over the factory at 200 feet, the aircraft bucking wildly in the explosions of its own bombs. By this time the whole target area was brightly lit with enemy searchlights, probing for the low-flying bomber, and the crew had no difficulty in finding objectives for their load of 20-lb Cooper bombs.

Lawson remained over the target for seven minutes, strafing the factory and searchlight batteries with machine-gun fire, then Purvis came in to bomb and strafe from the slightly safer altitude of 400 feet. A section of the works was put out of action for a fortnight, but the damage was limited by the failure of many of the bombs to explode.

Meanwhile, on 22 August, the Allied advance on the Somme had once more got under way. In preparation, No 3 Squadron AFC photographed the whole of the Australian Corps front on the 16th, while No 25 Squadron RAF flew similar sorties in the adjoining sector. Almost the whole of this operation was carried out twenty miles behind the enemy lines and the observation aircraft were subjected to heavy attacks, but all returned safely. During this period No 8 Squadron RAF, commanded by Major Trafford Leigh-Mallory – who was later to command No 12 Group in the Battle of Britain – made many experiments with wireless telephony, the main object of which was to enable the crew of an observation aircraft to direct a tank's crew, but nothing practical came of it.

The first British attack on 22 August, on a six-mile front between the Somme and the Ancre, was thwarted by a strong German counter-attack, but the next day the main attack in the battle for Bapaume began with an advance by the British 3rd and 4th Armies, supported by about 100 tanks. The British advanced some two miles, and on the 24th took the much-contested Thiepval Ridge and reached the outskirts of Bapaume. The principal objective was to take the high ground, and in this the British were successful. By 26 August their attack was spreading northwards along both banks of the River Scarpe, and twenty-four hours later the Anglo-French-American forces were advancing along the whole front. By the end of the month the Somme line had been decisively turned, twenty-three British divisions beating thirty-five German, taking 34,000 prisoners and capturing 270 guns.

Air operations during the last week of August were hampered by low clouds and rain, which helped to keep the Fokkers away from the observation aircraft, but the Germans were active during the breaks in the weather. Again, the record of No 3 Squadron AFC is fairly typical; at dawn on 23 August the RE8s were out in support of the 1st Australian Division, which was attacking strong German natural defences in the hilly, wooded positions around Chuignes, and by the morning of the 25th the aircrews reported that the Germans were withdrawing north of the Somme. Three RE8s, making a reconnaissance of the area near Péronne, came back with the news that it was deserted except for a few rearguards. During this phase of the battle No 3 Squadron shot down four enemy aircraft for the loss of one of its own, which crash-landed near Vauvillers.

The Germans withdrew to strong positions on the Somme bend at Péronne, the high ground near Bouchavesnes and St Quentin, and dug in. To keep the enemy on the run, the 2nd Australian Division crossed the Somme on 30 August, reaching Clery, and prepared to launch an attack the following morning. Wet weather now forced the observation pilots to fly very low and all had narrow escapes, but only one RE8 was lost. Attacked by thirteen enemy scouts, it was hit in the engine and had to make a forced landing in the Australian lines.

One of the most gallant fights during this period occurred on 29 August, when Lieutenant J. M. Brown and 2nd Lieutenant H. Lawrence, returning from a bombing raid in their No 98 Squadron DH9, fell behind the rest of the formation through engine trouble and were attacked by twenty Fokker D.VIIs. Almost immediately their elevator controls were shot away, but Brown somehow managed to retain control and dived towards the west, continually attacked by the enemy aircraft. Lawrence, although badly wounded, continued fighting and shot down a Fokker in flames, sending another down out of control soon afterwards. By this time all the DH9's petrol tanks were shot through, the engine hit in several places, and most of the instruments smashed. Lawrence, taking the brunt of the enemy fire in the rear cockpit, now had ten bullets in him; despite this he tried to keep on firing, but his guns jammed. Brown managed to evade the attacking aircraft by diving through a cloud and crash-landed near Mory. Brown later received a DFC, but there is no record of Lawrence receiving any award, nor indeed of what became of him; the inference is that he died of his very severe wounds.

On 27 August, a Sopwith Camel pilot was attacked by a Halberstadt; he promptly turned on it and fired 250 rounds into it, killing its observer, and the German aircraft spun down to crash. A few minutes later the same pilot attacked a Hannoveraner; its wings crumpled up and it went down to crash into a wood. The Camel pilot was Lieutenant W. R. 'Wop' May of No 209 Squadron, who had so narrowly escaped death at the hands of von Richthofen in April and who now had seven enemy aircraft to his credit. May scored a further victory in September, and was awarded the DFC.

Among the RAF's aces who added to their scores in the August battles was Raymond Collishaw of No 203 Squadron, who shot down three more enemy aircraft; he now had fifty-eight kills to his credit. Captain Beauchamp-Proctor of No 84 Squadron concentrated on balloon attacks during the month, but managed to shoot down a two-seater in flames on the 16th, followed by four more enemy aircraft later in the month; he was now the third surviving RAF ace after Bishop and Collis-haw, a South African following two Canadians. Next in line came another Canadian, Captain D. M. MacLaren of No 46 Squadron. The Irish ace, Captain G. E. H. McElroy, now had 47 kills, and was awarded the DFC during the month to add to his MC and Bar, but he was killed in action shortly afterwards.

On the Home Front, since the raid by Gothas and Giants in May, England had enjoyed more than two months of quiet. Then, on the night of 5/6 August, the Zeppelins of the German Naval Airship Division suddenly appeared on the scene, approaching the east coast and bound for the Midlands.

The last major Zeppelin raid against the British Isles, on the night of 19/20 October 1917, had been a disaster. Of the thirteen airships prepared for the attack, two had been pre-vented from leaving their hangar by a strong crosswind; the others, led by Lieutenant-Commander Peter Strasser – the head of the Naval Airship Division, and main architect of the attacks on Britain – had set course for the Midlands. One of them, the L.44, was shot down by French guns, all its crew of eighteen being killed; a second, the L.45, made a forced landing on French soil, its seventeen crew being captured; a third, the L.49, was brought down at Bourbonne-les-Bains following repeated attacks by fighters of *Escadrille* 152, its nineteen crew also being taken prisoner; and a fourth, the L.50, struck the ground during a rapid descent at Montigny-le-Roy. Part of the airship, with four men still inside, took off again and was lost somewhere over the Mediterranean; the other sixteen crew members became POWs. Of the ships that did successfully reach England, one, the L.55, crashed and burned at Tiefenort, Germany, on the way home. Because of the great height at which the Zeppelins flew over England, and because the defences were ordered to remain 'covered' in case gun flashes and searchlights gave away the position of the targets, the attack was known as the 'Silent Raid'.

Now, on this August night in 1918, the last Zeppelin raid of the war was also doomed to failure. Four of the five airships that had set out saw the fifth of their number suddenly blaze like a great torch in the darkness somewhere over the English coast. They dropped their bomb loads haphazardly, as far as sixty-five miles out to sea, and turned for home.

The Zeppelin that had been destroyed was the L.70. She was shot down by Major Egbert Cadbry, flying a DH4 from Great Yarmouth. She fell blazing into the sea with the loss of all her crew. Among them was the man who had striven to uphold the Naval Airship Division through four years of war, often in the face of adversity and criticism: Peter Strasser.

Four days later, the Germans lost another Zeppelin in somewhat historic circumstances. On 10 August, the Harwich Light Cruiser Force of the Royal Navy put to sea and set course towards the Heligoland Bight, where it was to conduct a 'special operation'. The force consisted of four light cruisers and eight destroyers, accompanied by six flying boats. The light cruisers carried six coastal motor-boats, whose task was to range the waters of the Bight at high speed and make torpedo attacks on any enemy shipping they encountered. The whole force was under the command of Vice-Admiral Sir Reginald Tyrwhitt, supervising the operation from his flagship, the cruiser HMS *Curacao*.

There was, however, another purpose behind the Harwich Force's penetration into enemy waters – a purpose centred upon a curious contraption towed behind one of the destroyers, HMS *Redoubt*. It was a lighter, with its top boarded over to make a platform of sorts, and perched precariously on the platform, lashed by the spray as the lighter bounced around in *Redoubt*'s wake, was a Sopwith Camel.

The idea was simple enough. During previous operations, the Harwich Force's operations had been hampered by the presence of Zeppelins, prowling over the warships at altitudes of up to 20,000 feet, where they were immune from naval gunfire and from interception by the floatplanes that the Force carried with it. The nearest British land base was Harwich, and no aircraft existed that possessed a 400-mile radius of action coupled with the ability to outclimb and outfight the airships. The logical step, therefore, was to convey fighter aircraft to a point where they would stand a reasonable chance of coming to grips with the enemy, hence the lighter-borne Camel.

In the early hours of 11 August, the ships of the Harwich Force began to transmit a series of fake wireless signals with the object of advertising their presence to the enemy. Admiral Tyrwhitt was confident that it would be enough to lure the

122

Zeppelins into the air in the morning, and the Camel's pilot would have the chance they were all waiting for.

The pilot in question, Lieutenant Stuart Culley, was feeling anything but confident. He had gained a fair amount of experience in flying off a pitching deck at Rosyth, where he had taken part in trials on the aircraft carrier HMS *Nairana*, but a thirty-foot lighter was a far different proposition. So far, only two attempts had been made to fly off a lighter; the first had ended in disaster when the Camel, piloted by Lieutenant-Colonel C. R. Samson, failed to attain flying speed and nose-dived over the front of the platform into the sea. Samson struggled out of the cockpit under water to find the lighter directly above him; somehow, he managed to claw his way from underneath it and come to the surface just in time. The second test, made by Culley himself, had been a success, but there were still a lot of snags attending the operation and only one or two had been rectified before the Harwich Force set sail.

The cruisers hove-to off the island of Terschelling at 5.30 am and lowered their six motor-boats into the water. Half an hour later, the little craft moved off at high speed towards the mouth of the River Ems. An attempt was made to launch three flying boats which, like Culley's Camel, had been towed with the Force on lighters; but there was a long swell, no wind, and the aircraft were too heavily laden with fuel and ammunition to take off under these conditions. The other three flying boats, covering the Force from their base at Great Yarmouth, had not yet arrived on the scene. When they did, at 7.20 am, they were ordered to patrol the enemy coast and search for the six motor-boats, which by this time were overdue.

In fact, the boats had run into serious trouble. Since 6.30 am they had been continually harassed by well-directed air attacks made by seaplanes of the German naval air squadrons at Borkum and Norderney; three boats were bombed and set on fire, while the other three came under heavy fire from the shore and ran aground.

The three Felixstowe F2A flying boats from Great Yarmouth failed to locate the motor boats, but shortly after 8.00 am the leader of the formation, Major Robert Leckie, spotted a Zeppelin approaching from the north-east at 15,000 feet. Not wishing to break wireless silence, he turned back and warned the Harwich Force of the airship's presence by visual signals. By similar means, he was informed that the Camel was being prepared for take-off; a minute later he was ordered to return to base and did so reluctantly, as his patrol was not yet half over.

The Zeppelin, the L.53, was sighted by the warships at 8.25, several miles away to the north-east. Admiral Tyrwhitt immediately brought the flotilla round in a wide turn and ordered the destroyers to lay a smoke-screen, hoping to lure the airship further out to sea. The L.53's commander, *Korvettenkapitän* Proelss, fell for the bait and followed the warships, the airship slipping in and out of cloud.

Far below, HMS *Redoubt* turned into wind and increased her speed to thirty knots. On the lighter behind her, Culley's ground crew clung to the Camel's wings and strove to keep their footing on the slippery platform. There were no hand rails. At 8.55 Culley, already soaked to the skin, gave a signal. A mechanic swung the Camel's propeller; his was the worst job of all, for in addition to the risk of falling overboard he would be chopped to pieces by the propeller blades should he lose his footing and stumble forward.

To everyone's surprise, the Bentley rotary burst into life at the first turn. One of the men holding the Camel down indicated that the shackles fastening the aircraft to the platform had been undone, and Culley opened the throttle. At another signal, the crew slid off the wings and threw themselves flat on the sodden deck. Free from any restriction, the Camel's tail came up immediately. Culley held the stick neutral and the thirty-knot wind did the rest; the fighter became airborne after a run of only five feet, seemed to hang motionless for a few seconds, and then started to gather speed.

With the sun behind him, Culley started the long climb towards the enemy. The Zeppelin had been clearly visible when he took off, but now he lost sight of it. As he climbed, he was dazzled by the effect of bright sunlight on a thin layer of haze. A film of ice began to form on his drenched clothing, and in spite of his thick flying combinations, the chill ate through to the bone.

At 9.15 the Camel suddenly burst through the haze and

Culley sighted the airship again, above and to the left. The distance between the two narrowed gradually, but at this height the Camel's rate of climb was painfully slow. Five minutes later the Zeppelin turned back towards the German coast, climbing as it did so; the crew must have seen the fighter, rising to intercept.

By 9.30 the Zeppelin was at 19,000 feet, with the Camel some 300 feet lower down, and Culley knew that if he was going to have any hope of success the attack would have to be made now, before the Camel reached its ceiling. It was already dangerously close to stalling. With the bulk of the airship seeming to fill the whole sky above him, he opened fire with the first of his two Lewis guns. After firing only fifteen rounds, it jammed. The pilot pulled the stick back into the pit of his stomach and opened up with the second Lewis, pouring a double charger of ammunition into the Zeppelin's envelope. A second later, the Camel stalled and spun away to the right.

Culley recovered and brought the fighter out of its dive, looking over his shoulder at the Zeppelin. A dull red glow was beginning to spread along the side of the L.53. He pushed the stick hard over and dived out of the way as the airship began to fall slowly, feeling the heat as it dropped past him. Seconds later, the Zeppelin was a fiery torch, burning from stem to stern as it fell vertically towards the sea three miles below. A tiny figure dropped away from the blazing bulk, tumbling over and over, its clothing alight. Fascinated, Culley watched as the burning mass plunged into the haze below.

A great cheer went up from the warships of the Harwich Force as the men saw the smouldering mass of girders and fabric that had been the L.53 tumble out of the murk and smack into the sea in a cloud of steam. Then, as the minutes went by, their elation changed to anxiety as Culley's aircraft failed to appear.

Above the haze, Culley was in trouble. For a start, he was unsure of his position. After cruising around for several minutes in a vain attempt to locate the British flotilla, he flew to the Dutch coast and turned south until he sighted Texel. Turning out to sea again, he went down to 6,000 feet, flying on a northerly heading towards the Terschelling Bank. But there was still no sign of the ships; patchy cloud now hid the water. Then, suddenly, the Camel's engine spluttered and died as the main fuel tank ran dry. Culley rapidly switched to the reserve tank and the motor burst into life again, but the secondary tank held only enough fuel for a further twenty minutes' flying. If he failed to sight the ships within the next couple of minutes, he would not have enough fuel to reach the Dutch coast again.

Looking down through a gap in the clouds, he spotted a Dutch fishing boat and decided to land in the sea beside it. Throttling back, he glided down – and then, emerging into a clear patch, he saw two destroyers. Close behind them came the whole flotilla.

Out of sheer relief, Culley looped and rolled his fighter over the warships for several minutes before curving down to make a perfect landing in the water ahead of HMS *Redoubt*. An hour later, with Culley safely aboard the destroyer and the Camel hoisted on to the lighter, the warships turned and set course for Harwich.

It was the second time in history that an enemy aircraft had been destroyed by a fighter launched from a vessel at sea. Almost exactly a year earlier, on 21 August 1917, Zeppelin L.23 had been shot down in flames off Lodbjerg, Denmark, by Flight Sub-Lieutenant B. A. Smart, flying a Sopwith Pup launched from a platform on HMS *Yarmouth*. Smart had come down in the sea and been picked up by the destroyer HMS *Prince*, but the Pup had been wrecked. On the other hand, Culley's action – for which he was later awarded the DSO – was significant because it marked the first time that a fighter and its pilot had been safely recovered after being launched by, and successfully providing air protection for, a naval force engaged in an operation against the enemy. It was to be nearly a quarter of a century before Culley's exploit was repeated, on a far greater scale, in European waters.

And on that August day in 1918, as the Harwich Force turned for home, Admiral Tyrwhitt made a curious signal to the flotilla. It read: 'Flag. General. Attention is drawn to hymn number 224, verse 7.'

When the sailors turned up the reference in their hymn books, they understood. For verse 7 of hymn 224 ran:

126

'Oh happy band of pilgrims
Look upwards to the skies,
Where such a light affliction
Shall win you such a prize.'

CHAPTER NINE

The third stage of the great British offensive on the Somme began on 2 September 1918, when the Canadian Corps of General Horne's 1st Army and the 17th Corps of General Byng's 3rd Army breached the enemy defences on a six-mile front between Drocourt and Quéant. On the following day, English, Scottish and Naval troops under General Fergusson smashed through the Quéant-Pronville defences. In those two days, the British forces took 34,000 German prisoners. The attacks were made in heavy rain and no real air support was possible until 8.00 am on the first day, but after that the army co-operation squadrons operated full out, bombing and strafing the retreating enemy as well as bringing back valuable information on their movements. Much depended on the success of the Canadian advance, which was followed throughout by two RE8s of No 13 Squadron; their reports enabled the commander of the 57th and 63rd Naval Divisions, on the flank of the Canadians, to commit his troops to action at exactly the right time, with decisive results.

In parallel with the British assault, General Mangin's French forces advanced to the north of Soissons. The *Cigognes*, as usual, were in the thick of the fighting; on 3 September Georges Madon scored his fortieth victory, a two-seater flown by *Vizefeldwebel* Max Sievert. By this time, most of the leading fighter units of the German Flying Corps had been concentrated in the Somme sector to meet the threat of the British advance, and the kills scored by the French pilots were mostly against observation aircraft or *Drachen* balloons.

The United States Army Air Service operated alongside the French. Early in September, Captain Eddie Rickenbacker was appointed to command the 94th Squadron; it was a bold decision on the part of his superiors, because other flight commanders were senior to him. Nevertheless, his all-round experience matched that of the others, and in some respects, such as technical skill, he excelled. He was also a very fine leader, a man who took the utmost care of the pilots he led into action. At this time, Rickenbacker had seven victories to his credit.

His superiors' faith in him was soon justified. He took over command of the 94th at a time when there was keen rivalry between it and its sister unit, the 27th Aero Squadron, and at the beginning of September the 27th had managed to creep ahead in the tally of enemy aircraft destroyed. This was a major source of annoyance to Rickenbacker, partly because the 27th was a newer unit than his own, and his first act on taking command was to assemble all the squadron personnel and deliver a strong pep talk. To the mechanics, he pointed out that the 27th's machines were seldom on the ground because of technical trouble, and that he expected to see a rapid rise in maintenance standards. From the pilots, he expected a comparable rise in the standard of tactics and teamwork; when they were not fighting they would train arduously until that standard had been reached.

It was tough stuff from a new commander, and had the words been delivered by anyone other than Rickenbacker they might have caused resentment. As it was, he achieved his object, and from that day the 94th set out to be better than any other unit. To prove his point, Rickenbacker set out on a lone patrol on 15 September. Over the lines he sighted two LVG two-seaters with an escort of five Fokker D.VIIs above and behind. Climbing into the sun, he dived on the Fokkers and shot one of them down. The others scattered, and Rickenbacker continued his dive on to the two-seaters. Running the gauntlet of fire from both enemy observers, he engaged the first LVG and then pulled up in a stall turn to repeat the attack. He carried out this manoeuvre several times, firing at each LVG in turn, and eventually got into a position to make a beam attack on the first LVG, keeping it between himself and the second enemy aircraft. He gave it a long burst and it went down in flames. Rickenbacker then broke off the attack and headed for home with the Fokkers still milling around in confusion overhead, having gained his eighth and ninth victories.

On 12 September the Americans had lost one of their leading aces. Lieutenant David Putnam, like many other Americans, had found his way into the Aviation Militaire by way of the French Foreign Legion, and had flown successively with SPA 94, 156 and 38. As a corporal, he destroyed his first enemy aircraft on 19 January 1918, and by July his score stood at eleven confirmed. He was then commissioned into the USAAS and assigned to the 139th Aero Squadron, with which unit he destroyed two more enemy aircraft on 15 and 22 August. On 12 September, during a patrol with Lieutenant Robertson in the St Mihiel area, he encountered six Fokker D.VIIs and, in the ensuing battle, was shot down and killed. His aircraft crashed at Limey and he was buried with full military honours at Toul.

In support of the French land offensive, the Aviation Militaire's bombers stepped up their daylight attacks on targets in western Germany, and they too encountered the formidable Siemens-Schuckert D.III. *Vizefeldwebel* Fritz Beckhardt, a pilot with *Kampfeinsitzerstaffel* 5 (No 5 Single-seat Fighter Squadron) at Lahr, described one encounter:

'At around 7.00 am we were suddenly alerted to deal with several enemy formations which had been reported approaching from the direction of Haguenau. We clambered into the cockpits of our D.IIIs and took off from the Lahr-Dinglingen airfield. We were not flying in formation, and our aircraft were scattered over a wide area. Suddenly, high above me, I saw two tiny specks. Aircraft flying on a north-easterly course at an altitude of 20,000-23,000 feet. I pulled back the nose of my D.III, opened the throttle fully and climbed after the intruders at full power. Owing to the superlative climbing performance of my aircraft, I was soon approaching the altitude of the enemy bombers, which I identified as Breguet 14s.

'When I reached an altitude only some 900 feet below the French aircraft, I loosed a couple of bursts from my machine-guns in an attempt to divert them from their target. One of the Breguets lost height rapidly. I put the nose of my D.III down a little in order to gain speed, caught up with the Frenchman and turned in to attack. Suddenly, a burst of machine-gun fire came from behind, and I hastily flung my D.III round in a climbing turn to find that the other Breguet had followed me down and had got on my tail. Out of the corner of my eye I noticed with satisfaction that the pilot of the crippled Breguet had apparently lost his sense of direction and was heading away from his own lines. A burst from my Spandaus put the gunner of the second Breguet out of action. I overshot the bomber, turned, and came up under my opponent, firing a long burst into the Breguet's belly. The Frenchman immediately went into a spin. I now turned my attention to the first machine which was still trying vainly to escape, but he proved easy meat, crashing into the river north of Kehl.'

In September, an improved model of the Siemens-Schuckert design also began to reach the German fighter squadrons. It had a completely redesigned upper wing and was designated SSW D.IV. The maximum speed, at 118 mph, was only slightly better than the D.III's, but the rate of climb was far better, the D.IV being able to reach 19,700 feet in sixteen or seventeen minutes. The first deliveries of the D.IV were made to *Jasta* 14, *Kampfeinsitzerstaffel* 2 at Saarbrücken, *Jasta* 22 and JG 2 Boelcke. A few were also assigned for home defence duties to the *Marine-Jagdgeschwader*, the German Navy's air defence wing. Lieutenant Alfred Lenz, commander of *Jasta* 22, reported that:

'The SSW D.IV is undoubtedly far superior to any single-seat fighter at the front today. This superiority manifests itself primarily in the climb rate and manoeuvrability of the fighter, and in maximum level speeds at altitudes above 13,000 feet.

'On 29 September, whilst on a sortie, I reached an altitude of 19,685 feet in 14.5 minutes. The time was carefully recorded by the cockpit chronometer and altimeter which were thoroughly checked for accuracy after completion of the sortie. During this sortie a British photo-reconnaissance aircraft and its escorting SE5 were outclimbed with the greatest of ease, and the SE5 shot down during a climbing turn.'

Fortunately for the Allies, the SSW D.IV came too late. Large orders were placed, but only 280 fighters of this type were delivered before the end of hostilities.

During the fighting on 2 September, a curious incident occurred which ended in a body of German troops surrendering to a British aircraft. Lieutenants Ibbotson and Carruthers, flying an RE8 of No 59 Squadron on the look-out for an enemy counter-attack, sighted sixty-five Germans huddled in a trench and a sunken road. The Germans fired at them, whereupon

Ibbotson dived and fired back, killing one and wounding three. As he turned to make a second attack, he saw that the enemy troops were waving a white flag. Throttling back, he descended to fifty feet and flew slowly past, he and Carruthers indicating by hand signals that the Germans were to head towards the British lines with their hands up. The enemy troops obliged, and the RE8 circled overhead until its crew were certain that they had been taken prisoner.

There were relatively few combats in the Somme area during the first week of September. The German pilots generally showed a lack of aggression, but on occasions showed flashes of their old determination. On 5 September, for example, the SE5s of No 92 Squadron fought a hectic battle with a strong formation of Fokker D.VIIs; the Squadron commander, Major A. Coningham (later Air Vice-Marshal Arthur Coningham, commander of the Desert Air Force in 1941-2) attacked the German leader's aircraft, which went into a steep climb and then fell over on its back. It seemed to hang motionless for a couple of seconds and the German pilot fell out. Coningham saw him hang desperately on to the edge of the cockpit for a while as the aircraft spun away, then he lost his grip and plunged to earth near Cambrai.

Meanwhile, Lieutenant Shapard, also of No 92 Squadron, had just shot down a D.VII when he was attacked from behind by several more. They gave him a hard time, and the only way he could escape was by putting his aircraft into a spin. He recovered almost at ground level and flew back to base at a height of twenty feet. On landing, he discovered how lucky he had been; the main spars of all four mainplanes had been shot through, his fuselage longerons were smashed and there was a bullet in one of his magnetos.

On the next day, a patrol of Fokker D.VIIs which attacked a flight of No 20 Squadron Bristol Fighters came off decidedly second best. One of the enemy aircraft passed directly in front of the Bristol flown by Captain H. P. Lale, who shot it down in flames, and at the same time a second Fokker was destroyed by his observer, 2nd Lieutenant H. L. Edwards. Lieutenant A. T. Iaccaci – one of the Americans in the RAF – meanwhile manoeuvred his Bristol so that his observer, Lieutenant A. Mills, could get in a series of effective bursts at more attackers;

Mills shot one to pieces in mid-air and saw another go down to crash, bursting into flames on impact. A fifth D.VII was shot down by Sergeant A. Newland, the observer in another Bristol.

Appallingly bad weather, with gale-force winds and heavy rainstorms, prevented all but the minimum of flying activity from 9 to 14 September, but after that the tempo of air fighting picked up once more. On 16 September, in the early hours, Lieutenant F. C. Broome of No 151 Squadron scored a notable success by shooting down a five-engined Giant bomber; after firing 500 rounds into it, he saw it burst into flames and fall on the British side of the lines. Two nights earlier, during one of the few spells when the wind dropped, Captain W. H. Haynes and Lieutenant E. P. Mackay, also of No 151 Squadron, had destroyed a Gotha apiece. The RAF's night-fighters were beginning to cost the enemy dearly.

During one of the early patrols on 16 September, Lieutenant W. T. Martin and Sergeant M. Jones, flying a Bristol Fighter of No 22 Squadron, attacked a formation of Fokker D.VIIs, one of which they shot down. They were then attacked in turn and had their aileron wires shot away; the Bristol side-slipped, almost out of control, through 2,000 feet. Sergeant Jones, with scant regard for his own safety, climbed out on to the bottom wing and stood there, clinging precariously to a strut, until his weight righted the aircraft. Martin was able to land the aircraft in friendly territory, and Jones was later awarded the DFM.

Another Bristol Fighter crew, Captain E. S. Coler and 2nd Lieutenant E. J. Corbett of No 11 Squadron, also had a lucky escape that day. While out on a reconnaissance they were attacked by a large number of Fokker D.VIIs, which shot away their aileron controls and put a bullet through one of their petrol tanks. Coler dived to 1,000 feet over Cambrai, still under attack, and two of the Fokkers overshot. Coler got behind one and shot it down; the other, which had turned quickly away and was not coming in for a stern attack, was shot down by Corbett. The Bristol Fighter staggered back across the lines at 150 feet and Coler, realizing that it was rapidly going out of control, used a combination of rudder, elevator and throttle to nurse it in a slow sidelip towards the ground. One set of wings struck first and absorbed most of the impact, the crew climbing from the wreck reasonably unharmed.

In fact, the Bristol Fighter squadrons appeared to bear the brunt of the enemy's attentions during this third week of September. On the 17th, Lieutenants Frank Jeffreys and F. W. Addison, out on reconnaissance in an aircraft of No 88 Squadron, were attacked by six Fokker D.VIIs. Addison shot down the first one, and another, which for one terrifying instant looked as though it was going to ram the Bristol, suddenly fell away on its back with part of its starboard wing in tatters. The remaining Fokkers harried the Bristol until it crossed the lines, one bullet grazing Addison's hand and putting his gun out of action. The aircraft landed with both its petrol tanks shot through.

On 20 September, Bristol Fighters of No 20 Squadron, together with SE5s of No 84 Squadron, fought a half-hour battle with twenty Fokker D.VIIs over St Quentin. Throughout the battle the RAF aircraft were at a great disadvantage because of a very strong westerly wind, which drove them progressively deeper into enemy territory. The Bristols quickly got the measure of their opponents; Lieutenant Harlock dived on one and shot it down, while his observer, 2nd Lieutenant Draisey, disposed of another. A second Fokker was shot down by Lieutenant Bolton and Sergeant Mitchell, and a third by Lieutenant McCall and 2nd Lieutenant Boothroyd. While the battle was in progress another Bristol Fighter, flown by Captain Middleton with Lieutenant Mills as his observer, arrived and joined in; they engaged in a merry-go-round with four Fokkers, two of which they shot down.

The fight was then joined by the SE5s of No 84 Squadron led by Captain Falkenberg, who immediately shot down one D.VII and drove another off the tail of a Bristol Fighter. Six more Fokkers were engaged by 2nd Lieutenant Nel, also of No 84 Squadron, who destroyed one and then escorted a damaged Bristol towards the lines. On the way home the pair were attacked by seven Fokkers and Nel was obliged to escape into a cloud; the Bristol Fighter failed to return.

On 16 September, the *Cigognes* suffered a grievous loss. Lieutenant Maurice Boyau had made a name for himself as a rugby star before the war, having played for France eleven times and captained the side; like so many others of his type he was naturally attracted to aviation, and by October 1917 he had ten victories to his credit – six balloons and four aircraft. (Unlike the British, the French counted observation balloons in a pilot's total of kills – a justifiable procedure, since attacking them was an extremely dangerous venture.)

Between 28 May and 4 June 1918 Boyau shot down five aircraft and two balloons, and by mid-July his score stood at twenty-nine. On 11 August he destroyed a balloon and a two-seater, then went off on leave, returning to the front on 13 September. In the next two days he shot down four more balloons; then, at 10.00 am on 16 September, he set out on an offensive patrol with a corporal named Walla. General Mangin's forces were fighting for the Chemin des Dames, and had requested the *Cigognes* to knock out some troublesome *Drachens*.

Neither pilot returned. Then, two days later, the news came in that Corporal Walla was lying gravely wounded in a French military hospital with an incendiary bullet in his back. He was able to give a few details of what had happened.

It seemed that Boyau had made three attacks on a balloon about six miles inside the enemy lines, sending it down in flames on his third pass. At that moment he and Walla were attacked by seven Fokker D.VIIs. Walla, obeying Boyau's earlier instructions, turned away and sped for the French lines, running the gauntlet of heavy machine-gun fire from the ground and pursued by the Fokkers. Boyau also turned, passing directly under the falling balloon, then pulled his SPAD round to engage the Fokkers while Walla made good his escape. Looking back, Walla saw Boyau's aircraft hit by ground fire; it burst into flames at once and went down to crash. Walla, wounded by a burst of fire from one of the Fokkers, managed to make a crash-landing in friendly territory.

The next day, the pilots of Boyau's unit, *Escadrille* SPA 77, arranged a rugby match. They played with fourteen men, and fourteen appeared on the photograph that was taken afterwards. Boyau's position was wing forward, and it was left vacant; but his name was recorded beneath it.

René Fonck, as usual, was on top form. On 26 September he destroyed six enemy aircraft in one day, the second time he had accomplished this feat. In the morning, flying from Chalôns-sur-Marne, he destroyed two Fokker D.VIIs and a two-seater; two more Fokkers and an Albatros fell to his guns in the afternoon. The Albatros broke up in mid-air and the pilot, tumbling from the cockpit like a sack of potatoes, narrowly missed hitting Fonck's SPAD. Fonck landed back at base trembling and soaked in sweat; the strain, at last, was beginning to tell. At this point, he had scored sixty-six victories.

By 24 September, the Allies were pushing against the last and greatest of the enemy's defences, the Hindenburg Line, which consisted of a vast network of concrete pillboxes, carefully sited trenches and barbed wire. Foch's plan was to attack it in four places, and allotted the sector running from St Quentin to Cambrai to the British. They faced a formidable task, for the St Quentin Canal had been incorporated as part of the defensive line and for a stretch of 6,000 yards it ran underground, providing excellent cover close to the front line for several thousand troops.

The assault was to be made by the 1st, 3rd and 4th British Armies, supported by over a thousand aircraft in twenty-seven fighter, four fighter-reconnaissance, seven day bomber, six night bomber and thirteen Corps squadrons. For several days prior to the offensive, the German night bombers made determined efforts to attack British supply dumps and other targets in the rear areas, and suffered heavily at the hands of No 151 Squadron's Camels. On 21 September Lieutenant F. C. Broome chased a Gotha in bright moonlight and opened fire from 200 yards. It fell in flames and disintegrated in the explosion of its own bombs. On the following night, Major Quintin Brand made a close-range attack on another Gotha, which went into a steep climb before falling over on its back and going into an inverted spin. Brand lost it, but British troops later confirmed that it had crashed near Gouzeaucourt. During the same patrol, Brand and another 151 Squadron pilot, Lieutenant J. H. Summers, attacked and destroyed a large enemy two-seater near Bourlon, and the Squadron's hat-trick that night was completed by Lieutenant A. A. Mitchell, who drove down a Gotha and saw it crash while attempting to land in a field.

On 24 September, when rain and low cloud gave way to a spell of fine weather, there was some intense air fighting as the RAF fighter squadrons battled to keep the enemy from the reconnaissance aircraft that were engaged in photographing the

Hindenburg Line defences. Other squadrons carried out bombing and strafing attacks on targets of opportunity behind the enemy lines, and it was during one of these on the 24th that Captain E. J. McCloughry of No 4 Squadron AFC nearly came to grief. He had just dropped a pair of 25-lb bombs on the rear part of a train, derailing it, when he was attacked by an enemy two-seater, which he shot down. He was then attacked by seven Fokker D.VIIs and wounded, but went on fighting. He got in a burst at one of the Fokkers, which broke up in mid-air, but then his ammunition ran out and he had no choice but to head for home as fast as he could. Two Fokkers got on his tail and he frightened them off by firing Very lights at them. McCloughry then passed out, and regained consciousness only just in time to right his aircraft and crash-land on the British side of the lines. This action, the culmination of months of gallant work by the Australian, earned him the Distinguished Service Order; he returned to command No 4 Squadron in October, having recovered from his wounds and been promoted major.

The other Australian fighter squadron, No 2, had a considerable success on 24 September, destroying five Fokker D.VIIs in one fight. A similar success was scored by No 148 (American) Squadron, which destroyed five out of seven D.VIIs in a dogfight over Bourlon Wood. One of the pilots who scored in this engagement was Lieutenant Field Kindley, who had shot down No 148's first German in July. Kindley survived the war with twelve victories, only to die in a flying accident at San Antonio, Texas, in 1920. The USAF's Kindley Air Force Base on Bermuda was named after him.

Airfield attacks were stepped up once again. On 26 September, eleven SE5s of No 40 Squadron and fourteen Camels of No 203, escorted by Bristol Fighters of No 22 Squadron, carried out a very low level attack on Lieu St Amand aerodrome. No 40 Squadron went in first, their bombs setting fire to a large hangar; then No 203 came in, setting four hangars ablaze and obtaining direct hits on some huts. During the attack, Major Raymond Collishaw spotted a Fokker D.VII taking off and shot it down; two DFWs were strafed on the ground by other pilots and left burning. On his way home, the RAF formation encountered a number of Fokker D.VIIs, two of which were shot down by a crew of No 22 Squadron and a third by Collishaw.

It was Collishaw's sixty-second and final victory. Soon afterwards he was sent back to Canada to help form the Royal Canadian Air Force, but this was delayed by the end of the war and so Collishaw remained in the RAF with a permanent commission. In November 1918 he was given command of No 47 Squadron, which he took to South Russia as part of the Allied Intervention Force, fighting for the Tsarist Russians under General Denikin. Following the collapse of that unhappy venture, Collishaw served in various commands until, in 1939, he was appointed Air Officer Commanding Middle East Bomber Group with the rank of Air Commodore. When the Italians entered the war he took command of No 204 Group, whose motley collection of aircraft he used to good effect in carrying out hard-hitting airfield attacks which thoroughly demoralized the enemy. Just how effective his scheme had been was revealed when the British forces invaded Cyrenaica and found over 1,000 Italian aircraft immobilized on their airfields, either wrecked in air attacks or starved of spare parts. He was promoted Air Vice-Marshal and, after a spell as AOC No 14 Group at Inverness, Collishaw retired in late 1943. After a successful career in business, he died in September 1976.

While the British were preparing to assault the Hindenburg Line, the Americans were on the offensive in the St Mihiel sector, and the last two weeks of September saw fierce fighting over that embattled area. Lieutenant Frank Luke was at last beginning to prove his qualities in action by destroying enemy observation balloons; he had now teamed up with another young pilot, Lieutenant Joe Wehner, and together they made a formidable pair. On 14 September, they set out to attack some balloons in the Buzy-Boinville sector; they were sited in an area that provided excellent observation for the enemy, and were strung up at an unusually low altitude. On this occasion, Luke and Wehner were escorted by six SPADs, whose pilots were detailed to provide top cover. It was just as well, for the Fokkers were lurking up above, as Luke's combat report tells:

'On arriving at Buzy, left formation and brought down enemy balloon in flames. While fixing my guns so I could attack another

138

balloon nearby, eight enemy Fokkers dropped down on me. Pulled away from them. They scored several good shots on my plane. I saw Lieutenant Wehner dive through enemy formation and attack two planes on my tail; but, as my guns were jammed, did not turn, as I was not sure it was an Allied plane until he joined me later.

'Left formation at Abaucourt and attacked an enemy balloon near Boinville. Dove at it six times at close range. Had two stoppages with left gun which carried incendiary bullets and, after fixing both, continued the attack. After about seventy-five rounds being left in right gun, I attacked an Archie battery at the base of the balloon. I'm sure that my fire took effect as the crews scattered. After my first attack on the balloon the observer jumped after he had shot at me. The last I saw of the balloon, it was on the ground in a very flabby condition.'

The next day, Luke and Wehner were ordered to bring down yet another balloon in the Boinville sector. As soon as they were over the front line they decided to split up and destroy as many balloons as their ammunition would allow, although this ran contrary to their orders. North-east of Verdun Wehner attacked a balloon and set it on fire with 100 rounds before being chased by five Fokkers; he was saved by the timely arrival of five French SPADs. He then turned towards the Bois d'Hingry, where another balloon had been reported, but Luke got there first and shot it down.

Wehner saw that Luke was being hotly pressed by seven Fokkers and Albatros DVs. Coming in behind them, he shot one down before the Germans realized he was there; as they broke in all directions he put a burst into an Albatros, seeing it go down to crash. Chased by the remaining enemy fighters, the two Americans pushed their noses down and raced for safety.

On 18 September, after destroying four more balloons between them during the two preceding days, Luke and Wehner were airborne again in search of new targets. Again, Luke's combat report tells what happened:

'Lieutenant Wehner and I left the airdrome at sixteen hours to spot enemy balloons. Over St Mihiel we saw two German balloons near Labeuville. Maneuvred in the clouds and dropped down, burning both. We were then attacked by a number of EA, the main formation attacking Lieutenant Wehner, who was above and on one side. I started climbing to join the fight when two EA attacked me from the rear. I turned on them, opening both guns on the leader. We came head on until within a few yards of each other when my opponent turned to one side in a nose dive and I saw him crash to the ground.

'I then turned on the second, shot a short burst, and he turned and went into a dive. I saw a number of EA above but could not find Lieutenant Wehner, so turned and made for our lines. The above fight occurred in the vicinity of St Hilaire. On reaching our balloon line, flew east. Saw Archie on our side, flew toward it, and found an enemy observation machine. I gave chase with some other SPADs and got him off from his lines. After a short encounter he crashed within our lines, south-east of Verdun. Lieutenant Wehner is entitled to share in the victories over both the balloons. Confirmations requested, two balloons and three planes.'

As soon as he got back to base, Luke went to seek out Joe Wehner. But Wehner would not be coming back; he had gone down in flames over Labeuville.

Luke was inconsolable, for Wehner was the only real friend he had ever had. His commanding officer sent him off on a fortnight's leave in Paris, but Luke returned after only a week, thirsting to be back in action. He sought and obtained permission to move up to an old French airfield closer to the front line. His new wingman was Lieutenant Ivan Roberts, and the pair made their first flight together on 26 September. Over Sivry they had a dogfight with five Fokkers; Luke sent one down out of control, but had to break off the fight when his guns jammed. On his return to base he found that Roberts was missing. The lieutenant was never seen again.

It was Joe Wehner all over again, and Luke was plunged into deeper gloom than ever. On 27 September he absented himself from his squadron and was gone until the following morning, when he returned and reported that he had paid a visit to the *Cigognes*. He also added that he had got another balloon.

His CO administered a severe reprimand, telling Luke that he was grounded until further notice. Luke went out in a rage and a few minutes later, despite his CO's order, he took off again, heading for the French airfield near Verdun. The day before, he had pinpointed the position of three more balloons,

140

and he was determined to get them, even though he knew that he might have to face a court martial when he returned.

Luke got his three balloons, but never had to face the court. Wounded in the shoulder by ground fire, he side-slipped down to land in a field. Climbing from the cockpit, he fought off advancing enemy troops with his revolver until they shot him dead. His last, gallant action was to earn him a posthumous Congressional Medal of Honor.

But the finest tribute to Luke's courage was paid by the man who had suffered most at his hands: Lieutenant Mangels, the commander of the balloon company in the Verdun sector. It was Mangels's machine-gunners who had shot Luke down, and he was one of the first officers to reach the scene, in the muddy field near Murvaux. Mangles ended his report on the incident with these words:

'His insignia I took and kept in remembrance of this great and fearless sportsman. He was a man of dazzling courage, one of the bravest we fought in the war.'

Meanwhile, at 5.30 am on 27 September, the British assault on the Hindenburg Line had begun. By nightfall, it was clear that the attack was meeting with success all along the line; the Canal du Nord had been crossed in several places and the enemy had lost 10,000 prisoners, as well as 200 guns. The part played by the RAF's army co-operation squadrons in this early victory was enormous; before the battle, an elaborate system of air-ground co-ordination had been worked out and rehearsed time and again between aircraft and artillery batteries, so that despite the swift movement of the battlefront the aircraft were able to direct the guns with great accuracy. Enemy aircraft were active along the battlefront, and the Corps squadrons came in for some punishment. Early on the 27th, for example, Lieutenant R. E. Britton and 2nd Lieutenant B. Hickman of No 13 Squadron, flying an RE8, were attacked by eight Fokker D.VIIs. Hickman was wounded early in the engagement but went on firing, sending one Fokker down out of control. A minute later Britton was wounded too, and in trying to take evasive action put the RE into a spin. He recovered just in time and landed in a field behind the German lines. As the Fokker circled overhead, the RAF men slumped in their cockpits and pretended to be dead. The ruse worked and the Fokker flew off without strafing the RE; as soon as it was safely out of sight Britton took off again and flew back to the Squadron's base at Mory, but passed out just as he was about to touch down and crashed. Both occupants were pulled from the wreck alive.

One RAF unit that was very active during the attack on the Hindenburg Line, and the period leading up to it, was No 79 Squadron, equipped with Sopwith Dolphins. No 79 was one of four squadrons on the Western Front to use the Dolphin – the others being Nos 19, 23 and 87 – and, after early misgivings, the pilots were discovering that it was an excellent combat aircraft. Designed as a Camel replacement, the Dolphin was unpopular at first with its pilots; the engine was virtually in the pilot's lap, with his face uncomfortably close to the butts of the overhead twin Lewis guns, he had a square steel-tube cockpit frame around his neck and the fuel tank was directly behind him. Nevertheless, the Dolphin was heavily armed; in addition to the Lewis guns, twin Vickers were mounted under the engine decking. Top speed was 120 mph, and ceiling was 19,000 feet.

In the week before the offensive No 79 Squadron destroyed nine enemy aircraft, four being shot down by 'A' Flight commander, Captain R. B. Bannerman. Then, on the 28th, the Squadron destroyed seven hostile machines in the course of the day, most of them in one battle during the afternoon when the pilots went to the rescue of a Bristol Fighter which was being attacked by ten Fokker D.VIIs. One was shot down by Lieutenant F. W. Gillet, who had also claimed a two-seater on an earlier patrol, two by Lieutenant J. McNeaney, and one each by Captain Bannerman, Captain F. I. Lord and Lieutenant F. Woolley.

The assault on the main Hindenburg Line defences, between Bellenglise and Vendhuille, was launched on Sunday 29 September. Captured German documents had provided the British commanders with details of every German defensive position, as well as supply dumps and communications centres, and these were subjected to heavy shelling and also bombing attacks as long as the weather permitted. Progress was swift – too swift in some areas, such as the sector in which the US 27th Division pushed on too far and found itself cut off in smoke and fog that made it impossible for pilots on contact patrol to see flares and other signals. As a result, the Americans suffered heavily. Bad weather on the last day of the month also made it impossible for the RAF to give full support to the ground forces, and enemy resistance was stubborn. Nevertheless, by nightfall on the 30th the British forces had taken the St Quentin Canal, almost all the Hindenburg Line defences had been over-whelmed, and German resistance was beginning to crumble. Soon, in the autumn rain and mist, clogged by the Flanders mud that had been the constant companion of millions of men for four years, the battered but still undefeated German armies were trudging back the way they had come in 1914.

CHAPTER TEN

As the Germans fell back step by step early in October, much of the Allied air effort was devoted to attacks on road junctions, railway stations and other bottlenecks. The German Flying Corps continued to fight fiercely, if spasmodically, and to inflict losses on the Allied day bombers, although in doing so their own losses were far from light.

On 1 October, for instance, DH9s of No 108 Squadron had just attacked Ingelmunster station when they were intercepted by thirty-three enemy scouts. A running fight developed, and in the next ten minutes, during which the DH9s managed to stay in close formation, they shot down four of the enemy without loss.

During the first week in October the two Australian fighter squadrons, No 2 with its SE5s and No 4 with its Camels, were very active, carrying out many ground-attack sorties against enemy airfields and lines of communication. No 4 Squadron in particular received several mentions in the official communiqués, beginning on 2 October:

'Lieutenants O. B. Ramsay and C. V. Ryrie, 4 Squadron AFC, left the ground at 4.45 am to attack Don Railway Station, where they dropped four 25-lb bombs, observing one direct hit; they then dropped four more bombs on Houplin Aerodrome and fired at machines and mechanics on the Aerodrome from 700 feet. A train steaming out of Haubourdin was also fired at and made to pull up.'

Then, on 5 October:

'A patrol of 4 Squadron AFC, consisting of Captain R. King, 2nd Lieutenant T. H. Barkell and 2nd Lieutenant A. J. Palliser, during a flight of 1 hour 20 minutes, carried out the following work: Destroyed one balloon in flames; dropped twelve 25-lb bombs from a low height on a train in Avelin Station and on the Aerodrome, obtaining four

144

direct hits on the station and one on a shed on the aerodrome. They also fired a large number of rounds into a "flaming onion" battery, and three times attacked horse transport, which scattered in confusion. The sheds on Avelin Aerodrome were also shot up, and finally a train was fired at, one wagon of which exploded, completely wrecking two trucks.'

In October a new German scout, the Fokker D.VIII, appeared at the front in small numbers. It was developed from the Fokker E.V, which had been assigned to *Jasta* 6 for operational trials in July but which had been withdrawn after three crashes involving structural failure of the wing. Imperfect timber and faulty manufacturing methods were found to have been the cause, and in September production was started again, the type now bearing the designation Fokker D.VIII. A parasol monoplane, the D.VIII was more manoeuvrable than the D.VII biplane and had a better operational ceiling, although it was slightly slower. Only about ninety had been delivered by the end of the war and, although its pilots reported that it handled well, it had little chance to prove itself in action.

With the end of the war in sight, and enemy aircraft absent from the front for lengthy periods, the leading Allied fighter pilots flew intensively, keen on adding to their scores. By the end of October, Eddie Rickenbacker of the 94th Aero Squadron had scored twenty-six victories, putting him well ahead of any other American pilot; the next in line was Captain W. C. Lambert of the RAF, with twenty-two, followed by Captain A. T. Iaccaci (RAF) and Frank Luke with eighteen, Captain F. W. Gillet (RAF) and Raoul Lufbery with seventeen, then Captains H. A. Kuhlberg and O. J. Rose (both RAF) with sixteen each. Rickenbacker survived the war to receive the Congressional Medal of Honor. After the war he was active in both the automobile and airline industries and was largely responsible for building up Eastern Airlines, of which he became chairman in 1953. During the Second World War he toured widely, visiting USAF units overseas. In one flight across the Pacific his aircraft had to ditch, and he and his crew spent twenty-one days on a life-raft before being rescued. He remained active in various fields until his death in July 1973, at the age of eighty-two.

145

In the *Cigognes*, René Fonck scored his sixty-eighth and sixty-ninth victories on 5 October. There was no one to come near him now, but sightings of enemy aircraft were so infrequent that it would be the end of the month before he scored again.

Meanwhile, in the north, the RAF took its latest fighter, the Sopwith Snipe, into action during these final weeks. No 43 Squadron had begun offensive patrols with its new Snipes on 26 September; these mostly involved bomber escort or diversionary patrols in conjunction with bombing raids, and in six days the pilots claimed the destruction of ten enemy aircraft for no loss. Unfortunately, only two of the enemy machines could be confirmed, these being credited to Lieutenants E. Mulcair and R. S. Johnston. Throughout October No 43 continued to fly escort missions, often with the DH9s of Nos 98 and 107 Squadrons. On occasions the Snipe pilots would also indulge in some bombing; on 23 October, for example, they obtained several direct hits with 20-lb Cooper bombs – four of which could be carried beneath the Snipe's fuselage – on the railway station at Hirson.

In October a second unit, No 4 Squadron Australian Flying Corps, also began to exchange its Camels for Snipes at Serny. The first patrol with the new aircraft was flown on the 26th, when nine Snipes led by Lieutenants T. C. R. Baker and T. H. Barkell ran into fifteen Fokker D.VIIs over Tournai. Barkell, although wounded in the leg, shot down two of the enemy, while Lieutenants Baker, E. J. Richards and H. W. Ross got one each. On the following day the Squadron lost Lieutenant F. Howard, shot down and killed in a dogfight over the same area.

The next three days saw some of the greatest air battles of the war as the German Flying Corps threw its dwindling reserves into action against the Allied aircraft that were now swarming everywhere behind the enemy lines. On 28 October, fifteen Snipes of No 4 Squadron AFC, led by Captain A. T. Cole, came upon twelve Fokker D.VIIs which were attacking a formation of DH9s over Peruwelz and destroyed five of the enemy for no loss. Later in the day, ten Snipes under Captain R. King were detailed to escort twelve SE5as of No 2 Squadron AFC in a bombing attack on Lessines, north of Ath on the

Dendre river. The SEs carried out their bombing attack and then climbed to join the Snipes, which were engaging about thirty Fokkers. By the time the SEs arrived the fight was virtually over; two of the Fokkers had been destroyed by Lieutenant A. J. Palliser, a third by Major W. A. McLaughry and a fourth by Lieutenant T. C. R. Baker, who had already shot down a D.VII while out on patrol by himself that morning. Another Fokker was destroyed by Lieutenant E. L. Simonson of No 2 Squadron, who shot the enemy off a Snipe's tail.

In the afternoon of 29 October, fifteen Snipes of No 4 Squadron in two flights under King and Baker were patrolling near Tournai in fine but hazy weather when they encountered an equal number of Fokker D.VIIs at 14,000 feet. Conscious that there were other strong formations of Fokkers in the area – probably sixty aircraft in all – the Australians quickly engaged the first gaggle, which were apparently preparing to attack some Allied two-seaters lower down. A fierce battle ensued, during which two Fokkers were shot down in flames by Lieutenant G. Jones. Two more were destroyed by Lieutenant Palliser, while Lieutenants Baker, P. J. Sims, O. Lamplough and H. W. Ross accounted for one each. Unfortunately, Sims failed to return from this fight.

On 30 October, the bomb-carrying SE5as of No 2 Squadron AFC joined other aircraft in an attack on Rebaix airfield. The bombs were dropped from a very low altitude – sometimes as low as twenty feet – destroying several hangars and buildings as well as three LVG two-seaters parked nearby. The raid was escorted by eleven Snipes of No 4 Squadron, but no enemy aircraft were sighted.

There followed a spell of poor weather which finally broke on 4 November, when No 2 Squadron AFC formed part of a force that carried out a highly successful attack on Wattines airfield. The raid, which was escorted by No 4 Squadron AFC and the Bristol Fighters of No 88 Squadron RAF, was hotly contested by the enemy, and in the running battle that developed six Fokkers were shot down. But it was a bad day for No 4 Squadron: Lieutenant Goodson was hit by anti-aircraft fire, crashing into the canal at Tournai, and Lieutenant C. W. Rhodes was shot down in combat, both airmen surviving to become prisoners. They were luckier than Captain T. C. R.

Baker and Lieutenants Palliser and P. W. Symons, all of whom were shot down and killed.

It was a hard loss for the Australians to bear, with the end so near. The Germans were now in full retreat from the Scheldt, and in the days that followed both Australian squadrons were engaged in attacks on enemy forces near Ghislenghien, rolling stock at Enghien and on Croisette airfield. No opposition was encountered in the air, and so the Snipes of No 4 Squadron came down to join the SEs in strafing attacks. The last offensive sortie by the Australian Snipes was carried out on 10 November, when enemy columns were strafed in the Enghien area.

The sturdy Snipe had fulfilled all its expectations in the hands of the Australians; but it was the extraordinary exploit of a Canadian pilot, Major W. G. Barker, that was to enshrine the fighter in aviation history during those last weeks of the war.

Bill Barker had arrived in France in 1915 with the Canadian Mounted Rifles, and after spending his twenty-first birthday in the mud of Flanders had applied for a transfer to the RFC. Accepted as an air gunner with the lowly rank of Air Mechanic, he had been posted to No 9 Squadron RFC, which in the closing months of 1915 was flying BE2c observation aircraft from Allonville. He was an expert shot, having hunted elk from horseback as a boy, and his skill was rewarded when he destroyed a Fokker monoplane that attacked his BE behind the enemy lines.

Early in 1916, Barker was commissioned and posted to No 4 Squadron RFC, which also flew BEs, as an observer. After taking part in the air operations over the Somme, during which he was slightly wounded in a skirmish with an enemy fighter, he applied for pilot training in the autumn of 1916. He was awarded his pilot's brevet in January 1917 and posted as a captain to No 15 Squadron, flying on artillery spotting duties. He survived the bloody fighting of 1917 and was awarded the Military Cross; in September he was posted to No 28 Squadron, which took its Sopwith Camels to France in October. He was given command of 'C' Flight, and adopted Sopwith Camel serial number B6313 as his 'personal' aircraft. Together, pilot and machine were to make a formidable team.

His first victory with No 28 Squadron came on 20 October 1917, when he shot down an Albatros near Roulers. This was followed, six days later, by two more. These were Barker's last victories in France for the time being, for in November No 28 Squadron was sent to the southern front as part of the Allied effort to bolster the Italians, who had suffered a series of reverses in their campaign against the Austrians. When Barker went to Italy, so did his faithful B6313.

Barker shot down an Albatros on 29 November and another on 3 December, the first of nine victories he was to score with No 28 Squadron on the Italian Front. On 8 March 1918 B6313 was damaged when it crash-landed in mist at Asolo, but it was flying again a week later and Barker celebrated the Camel's return to action by destroying an Albatros D.III at Villanova on 18 March, followed by another near Cismon the next day.

On 10 April 1918 he was posted to command No 66 Squadron at San Pietro, and once again he took B6313 with him. By 13 July his score stood at twenty eight enemy aircraft and four observation balloons destroyed. One of his victims during this period was *Oberleutnant* Frank Linke-Crawford, the third-ranking Austrian ace with thirty victories.

On 14 July 1918 Barker was promoted Major and given command of No 139 Squadron, which was then flying Bristol Fighters at Villaverla. Once again, his Camel went with him; to keep the paperwork straight, it was officially transferred to 'Z' Aircraft Park, which was a maintenance unit, and attached to No 139 Squadron. Barker had it painted in the markings of No 139: multiple narrow white stripes applied vertically between the fuselage roundel and the tailplane.

Although Barker flew Bristol Fighters on some occasions, he usually accompanied the two-seaters in his B6313, and while flying this aircraft he destroyed six more enemy machines, the last on 18 September 1918 over the Piave front. The useful life of B6313 was now coming to an end; the Camel had already been re-engined several times, and its airframe was showing dangerous signs of wear and tear. Accordingly, the commander of the RAF contingent in Italy, Colonel P. B. Joubert de la Ferté (later Air Chief Marshal Sir Philip Joubert de la Ferté KCB, CMG, DSO), directed that the aircraft be dismantled and the pieces placed in storage for spares; Major Barker was to be allowed to take any souvenirs he wished. As a long-standing fighting partnership between one man and one aircraft, it was probably unique.

At the beginning of October 1918 Barker returned to the United Kingdom and was posted to No 201 Squadron at La Targette. The Squadron was then still equipped with Sopwith Camels, but was due to receive Snipes in the near future. One Snipe, serial E8102, was allocated to Barker for use in the Squadron; his overall brief was to test the aircraft to the fullest extent in action and to develop new air fighting techniques.

By the time he joined No 201 Squadron, Barker's score of aircraft destroyed stood at forty-six. His decorations included the DSO and Bar, MC and two Bars, the *Croix de Guerre* and the Italian Cross of Valour. He was just twenty-four years old.

Barker's time with No 201 Squadron, however, was short-lived, amounting to little more than a refresher course, and in the last days of October he was ordered back home to take up a new and safer posting as CO of a flying school at Hounslow in Middlesex. On the morning of the 27th, he took off from La Targette for the last time and set course westwards towards the English Channel.

Suddenly, as he cruised high over the Forêt de Mormal, something caught his attention: a flicker in the sky, several thousand feet higher up. It was the wing of a turning aircraft, glittering in the sun, and Barker knew that in this area the chances were that it was a Hun. He decided to climb up and investigate.

The strange aircraft turned out to be a Hannoveraner two-seat observation aircraft, flying at 21,000 feet. At this altitude, which was well above the normal patrol level, its crew possibly thought that they were immune from attack. Nevertheless, the enemy observer was wide awake, and put a burst of Spandau bullets through the Snipe's wing as Barker closed in to make his attack. The Canadian fired back and saw his bullets strike home, but the Hannoveraner flew steadily on. Twice more the Canadian closed in, exchanging bursts of fire with the enemy gunner. Both aircraft were hit repeatedly. Suddenly, Barker decided to change his tactics. Long ago, he had removed the conventional radial sight from his twin Vickers machine-guns and replaced it with a simple peep sight, which he claimed was more accurate. He now concentrated on hitting the German gunner, and after a burst or two saw the man throw up his arms and collapse in the cockpit.

The German aircraft was defenceless now, and Barker closed in to finish it off from point-blank range. After a few moments it broke up, its fuselage spinning down towards the forest and its wings drifting in the air. It was Barker's forty-seventh victory.

Elated, he did not see the Fokker D.VII coming up under his tail. The first indication of its presence came with a confused sensation of whiplash cracks as bullets spattered his aircraft, followed by a spasm of searing pain as one of them tore into his right thigh. The Snipe fell into a spin which Barker corrected by instinct, half dazed with the shock of his wound. Looking round, he found that he had dropped into the middle of a formation of about fifteen more Fokkers and immediately flung his Snipe into a steep turn, loosing off an inconclusive burst at an aircraft that flashed across his nose. He fired at a second, again with no apparent result, but almost at once found himself on the tail of a third.

This time there was no mistake. There was a short burst from Barker's guns and the Fokker trailed a short stream of white fuel vapour before bursting into flames and rolling earthwards in a ball of fire.

By this time, the Germans were queueing up for a shot at Barker's twisting aircraft. Bullets crackled around his ears and ripped savagely through the Snipe's wings and fuselage. Two Fokkers attacked simultaneously from behind. Barker throttled back and hammered one of them as it flashed past, seeing part of the enemy's tail break away. Then another Fokker came up from below and fired a burst into the underside of the Snipe. Bullets shattered Barker's left leg and he blacked out. The Snipe nosed over into a dive, and the rush of icy air brought the pilot round. At 12,000 feet he managed to pull the aircraft out of its plunge.

The Snipe creaked and groaned alarmingly, and smoke poured from its overworked engine. When another Fokker came at him head-on, Barker, thinking that his aircraft was on fire, weak as he was through loss of blood and with both his legs smashed, made up his mind to ram it. Then, almost at the last moment, he saw an opportunity and opened fire. The

151

Fokker disintegrated in a cloud of fragments and Barker flew unscathed through its floating wreckage.

Suddenly, Barker realized that his left arm was useless. Looking down, he saw that his sleeve was soaked with blood; a bullet had shattered his elbow. For the second time in this incredible, one-sided battle, Barker fainted.

Again, it was the rush of slipstream that brought him to his senses. Pulling out of the dive, he saw his avenue of escape cut off by eight more Fokkers, which split up to attack him from several directions. One Fokker made a fatal mistake and turned in front of him; Barker's guns chattered again and the enemy aircraft went down to crash. Resigned now to the fact that he was going to be shot down by the others, he fired his remaining ammunition at them. Miraculously, they broke off the action and flew away eastwards.

Barker, his strength failing rapidly, dived to within a few feet of the ground. Both his legs and his left arm were completely useless, preventing him from using the rudder bar. Somehow, he managed to keep a firm grip on the control column as the tattered, smoking, oil-slicked wreck of the Snipe sank lower. Finally, the wheels struck the ground with a jarring crash; the Snipe bounced into the air and fell on its back. By some miracle it failed to catch fire.

The aircraft had crashed near some British observation balloons, whose ground crews pulled him barely alive from the wreckage. He was taken to Rouen hospital and was still there, deeply unconscious and fighting for his life, when the Armistice came. He eventually went on to make a full recovery, and to receive one of the best-earned Victoria Crosses in the history of air warfare. Sadly, he was killed while working as a test pilot in 1930, at the age of thirty-six.

While Barker lay in hospital, the war entered its last days. After 4 November, a day of intense air fighting, the RAF's daily summaries noted that enemy air activity was slight; sometimes it was absent altogether. Officially, between 4 and 11 November, the RAF claimed sixty-eight enemy aircraft destroyed and twenty-four 'driven down out of control' for the loss of sixty of its own.

In the last hours of the war, the weather was fair but misty. During the night of 10/11 November, No 214 Squadron's

Handley Page 0/400s dropped 112 bombs on Louvain railway sidings, the crews reporting many direct hits. Some of the bombs hit an ammunition train, causing explosions and fires all over the sidings.

At 11.45 am on 11 November, an RE8 observation aircraft of No 15 Squadron touched down at Auchy. Its crew, Captains H. L. Tracy and S. F. Davison, reported that no enemy aircraft had been seen; British troops were in Mons, where the British Expeditionary Force's long retreat had started more than four years earlier, and enemy AA fire was nil.

On the Western Front, at last, all was quiet.

EPILOGUE

And so it was over. Over for the Richthofen *Geschwader*, its war career ended in a terse footnote to the final report written by its commander, Hermann Goering:

'November 11th. Armistice. Squadron assembled at Darmstadt in bad weather. Fog.'

Over for Captain John Pattern who, after his victory against Erwin Boehme in November 1917, had himself narrowly escaped death when, during a night bombing raid on Menin and Courtrai in February 1918, he had been badly wounded in the head by shrapnel and only just made it back to his airfield, where he had crashed on landing. The end of the war found him instructing with an artillery observation school at Old Sarum in Wiltshire, and the three flights entered on his log-book for 11 November are followed by the remarks 'Aerobatics – aerobatics – aerobatics: PEACE DAY!'

Over for Captain Cecil Lewis, formerly of the celebrated No 56 Squadron, but now with No 152 near Lille. He wrote:

'I confess to a feeling of anti-climax, even to a momentary sense of regret. We were a new squadron, fresh overseas, we wanted – particularly the new pilots – to justify our existence, to carry out in action the thing we had been training for. Moreover, when you have been living a certain kind of life for four years, living as part of a single-minded and united effort, its sudden cessation leaves your roots in the air, baffled and, for the moment, disgruntled. But the readjustment was rapid and soon we began to explore the possibilities of peace. Where should we go? What should we do?'

The same thoughts undoubtedly passed through the minds of Georges Madon, and Charles Nungesser, and René Fonck on that day in November. Madon had scored his forty-first and last

154

victory on 30 October, when he destroyed a Fokker D.VII flown by Sergeant Ludwig Pfluger near Dizy-le-Gros. He remained in the *Aviation Militaire* and was posted to Tunisia. It was there, on 11 November 1924, that he took off for the last time to carry out an aerobatic display in connection with the Armistice Day celebrations. No one knows how, or why it happened; but Madon's aircraft plunged to the ground at Tunis and he was killed instantly. His body now lies in the cemetery at Bagneux, on the outskirts of Paris.

Nungesser, his body still suffering from the ravages of war, formed his own aviation company after the war – as did so many others of his kind – and flew wherever there was money to be made from flying. On 8 May 1927, together with Francois Coli, his navigator, he took off from Paris in an attempt to cross the Atlantic from east to west. The aircraft was a Levasseur named '*L'Oiseau Blanc*' (The White Bird) in memory of the *Cigognes*, and on its side it carried a macabre emblem, derived from a degree in Freemasonry, that was Nungesser's personal symbol, one which had been painted on his fighter during the war: a heart bearing a skull and cross-bones, a coffin and two funeral candles.

The aircraft took off safely, and as soon as it was airborne Nungesser jettisoned its undercarriage – a measure designed to save weight and cut down drag, for the Levasseur would have to fly into the teeth of the prevailing westerly wind. A small armada of aircraft accompanied it as far as the English Channel, then it continued alone until it was lost to sight against the western sky.

It vanished without trace, somewhere out there over the grey Atlantic wastes. All that remained of it was its undercarriage, preserved today in France's *Musée de l'Air*.

And there was Fonck. In the forty-eight hours between 30 October and 1 November France's ace of aces destroyed six enemy aircraft, the last a Halberstadt CII which, crewed by Lieutenant Fischer and Sergeant Jeromin, was dropping prop-aganda leaflets on French positions at Vouziers. It was his seventy-fifth victory.

After the war, Fonck took up a career in civil aviation. In the spring of 1920, while attending a banquet in Stockholm to mark the occasion of the founding of a Swedish airline, he had a curious experience. One evening after dinner, there was a telephone call from someone who would only identify himself as a former member of the Richthofen *Geschwader*. It turned out to be Hermann Goering, its last commander, who like many others had left the chaos of post-war Germany and for some time had been eking out a living by giving pleasure flights. Now, desperately anxious to get a job in commercial aviation, he asked Fonck to put in a good word for him. The French ace, anxious to help a fellow pilot and former adversary, did not hesitate. He dropped a word in the right quarter, and Goering got a job with the new airline.

Years later, this incident was to have unforeseen repercussions. Following the Franco-German armistice of June 1940, Fonck – who then had the rank of Lieutenant-Colonel in the *Armée de l'Air* – was summoned to Vichy by Marshal Philippe Pétain, who asked the pilot if he would visit Goering, exploit his old contact, and try to sound out Hitler's intentions with regard to the future of Vichy France.

As Pétain's emissary, Fonck visited Goering several times during the next two years, and the two became friendly. In 1945, however, when the leaders of Vichy France were placed on trial, some of the mud thrown at them inevitably stuck on Fonck. Almost overnight, he fell from his status as a national hero to something approaching a criminal; old friends avoided him, forgetting his former exploits – just as France conveniently forgot that Pétain himself had been the 'Hero of Verdun' in the former war. And so René Fonck died a bitter, broken man, his star eclipsed by spite and bitterness in a world that knew nothing of the wind in the wires, or the taut drumming of fabric on an aircraft's wing.

For some, the fighting did not end in November 1918. In March 1919, No 47 Squadron RAF, with two flights of DH9s and one of Camels – all war-weary and poorly maintained – arrived at Beketovka in south Russia to support the Tsarist forces in their fight against the Bolsheviks. Two days after its arrival, the news came that the Reds had brought up numbers of aircraft to nearby airfields, many of them German types left behind in the German withdrawal from the Ukraine. It was also believed that they were being flown in some cases by experienced German pilots – men who, their wings clipped by the Armistice, had offered their services as mercenaries.

No 47 Squadron was asked to make a reconnaissance beyond Tsaritsyn. It was carried out by four Camels led by Major Marcus Kinkead, a South African ace with thirty-six victories who was later to lose his life in 1927 while trying to break the world air speed record over the Solent in a Supermarine S.5 floatplane. One Camel, flown by Captain Aten, an American, turned back with engine trouble and was attacked by a Nieuport fighter, which missed and overshot. Aten dived after it and opened fire at fifty yards; the Nieuport dived into the bank of the Volga and exploded. It was No 47 Squadron's first victory in Russia.

The Squadron was in action again the following day, escorting a formation of 'A' Flight DH9s in a raid on the Bolshevik HQ at Tsaritsyn. Two enemy fighters, a SPAD and a Fokker Triplane, came up to intercept, but the SPAD was immediately shot down and the Fokker broke off the engagement.

In May 1919, No 47 Squadron was ordered to step up its operations and destroy as many enemy aircraft as possible in support of the White Russian advance on Tsaritsyn. During the first ten days of the month the squadron destroyed seven enemy aircraft; many of the latter were operating from an airfield near Urbabk, and in the second week of May this was attacked by White Russian DH9s escorted by the Camels. The Reds came up in strength to intercept with a mixed formation of Nieuports, SPADs and an Albatros, the whole led by an all-black Fokker D.VII.

A whirling dogfight spread across the sky as the Reds attacked with a determination the British pilots had not encountered previously. The black Fokker destroyed two DH9s, then circled overhead as the remainder of his squadron engaged the Camels. The British pilots got the best of the encounter, shooting down five enemy aircraft, but all the Camels were damaged and Major Kinkead had to make a forced landing on the bank of the Volga with a shot-up engine.

Throughout that summer the squadron flew intensively, the pilots seeing early White Russian victories gradually crumble into defeat. There was a marked decrease in enemy aircraft activity, a number of the Red squadrons having been withdrawn for service on other fronts. Nevertheless, the Reds appeared in strength from time to time. On one occasion in August, an RE8 observation aircraft, escorted by two Camels, was attacked over the Volga by two enemy machines. One was a Nieuport, and the other was the all-black Fokker D.VII which had already been encountered on several occasions.

While the RE8 put its nose down and headed for home at top speed, the two Camel pilots – Captains Aten and Burns-Thompson – engaged the Red aircraft, Burns-Thompson taking on the Nieuport and Aten the Fokker. After a savage dogfight that lasted several minutes both enemy aircraft were shot down, and a second Nieuport that joined the fight was also destroyed by Aten. Later, General Wrangel, the White Russian commander, telegraphed his congratulations; the pilot of the black Fokker had destroyed at least a dozen bombers during his short career in the Russian Civil War.

Privately, the pilots of No 47 Squadron suspected that his score might be much higher than that. The tactics he had used, the flair he had shown, were of the kind they had all encountered on so many occasions, when they had faced the elite pilots of the Richthofen and Boelcke *Geschwader* over the Western Front.

But no one ever found out who he was.

INDEX

168

169

172